French Bulldogs — Frenchies

Owners Guide from Puppy to Old Age

Choosing, Caring for, Grooming, Health, Training, and
Understanding Your French Bulldog

By Alex Seymour

Copyright and Trademarks

Disclaimer and Legal Notice

Foreword

French Bulldogs have resurged in popularity in recent years because they are the perfect size to live as apartment dogs, are extremely affectionate with their owners, exhibit a high level of intelligence, and are so darn cute it's almost impossible not to croon "awwwwwwww" when you see one.

For me, it was love at first sight and I've been owned by several Frenchies since that time.

That being said, I really wouldn't recommend the breed for everyone. French Bulldogs are reasonably healthy dogs when acquired from a reputable breeder, but they are, to some extent, what my grandfather derisively called "hothouse dogs."

That's actually a misnomer. They're more "air conditioner" dogs. Frenchies don't do well in temperature extremes, cannot take vigorous exercise, and they can't swim (unless taught how to). This all works for me. I live in a small space. I like to get the dog walking over in the cool of the day and not be gone more than a few minutes. I live in a climate where I prefer an air conditioner as well — and I work from home.

My Frenchie is perfectly happy to get up with me, make a quick circuit around a couple of blocks, and then settle into his favorite bed to supervise me for the rest of the day. This is punctuated by a little in-house play and a lot of snoring on his part.

He's not a big barker, although he holds a personal grudge against the UPS man which I've never quite been able to fathom.

When my little tyrant doesn't like something I do, he's much more likely to let out a warbling yodel to express his displeasure, which I frankly find funny. I'm not sure the neighbors would agree.

I like the breed's highly social nature and easygoing spirit. They can be, by turns, quite comical, and they are very faithful. My little guy does have a minor subluxating patella, which we are managing, and thankfully no hip dysplasia, which is a known issue with the breed.

In the following pages, I will try to acquaint you with all the pros and cons of life with a Frenchie and to provide insight into canine husbandry for those people who have not lived with a dog before.

I do think a Frenchie is a good "first dog" and they will get on famously with well-behaved children, but they can't take a lot of outside rough housing.

Read carefully and make your decision with a critical eye toward your time and lifestyle. I firmly believe that no adoption of any animal should be based on any primary consideration other than the welfare of the living creature that will become your primary responsibility. If you can care for a Frenchie, I promise, the Frenchie will care for you.

As an owner, expert trainer, and professional dog whisperer, I would like to teach you the human side of the equation, so you can learn how to think more like your dog and eliminate behavioral problems with your pet.

Once you've read this book you will have all the information you need in order to make a well-informed decision about whether or not the French Bulldog is the breed for you, and you will know how to care for them every stage of their life.

Acknowledgments

In writing this book, I also sought tips, advice, photos, and opinions from many experts of the French Bulldog breed.

In particular I wish to thank the following wonderful experts for going out of their way to help and contribute:

Stephen Miller of Péché Mignon French Bulldogs
http://www.pechemignonfrenchbulldogs.com

Karen Fore-Monroe of Fancibul French Bulldogs
http://www.fancibul.com/

Necia Metzger of Metzger's Bulldogs
http://metzgersfrenchbulldogs.com/

Kathi Liebe of Starcreek Frenchies
http://www.starcreekfrenchies.com

Richard & Michelle Shannon of Smokey Valley Kennel
http://www.smokeyvalleyfrenchbulldog.com

Mary Schroeder of FleetFire French Bulldogs
http://fleetfirefrenchbulldogs.com/about/

Bev Anderson of Timepieces French Bulldogs Perm Reg'd
http://timepiecesfrenchies.com

Debbie Ecarius of Suirac French Bulldogs
http://www.suiracfrenchbulldogs.com

Susan L. Neidlinger of Crusader French Bulldogs

The owners of Sir Charles Barkley and Manny.

Table of Contents

Table of Contents

Table of Contents

Table of Contents

Table of Contents

Table of Contents

Table of Contents

Table of Contents

Chapter 1 – All About the French Bulldog

As pets, French Bulldogs, or "Frenchies" as they are lovingly known, are active and alert, displaying well-balanced dispositions. They are not overly rowdy dogs, and are smart and wonderfully affectionate.

French Bulldogs are an excellent and attractive companion breed, and a perfect size for people living in smaller spaces, like apartments. They get on exceptionally well with children, and with people who are disabled or elderly.

Frenchies, in an unusual, but particularly lovely trait, seem to know how to match their energy and level of activity to meet the needs of the people with whom they are living or interacting. For this reason, French Bulldogs are often selected to be therapy dogs and excel in this work.

"Frenchie" History

In the early 1800s, British Bulldog fanciers in England began to work on cultivating a toy version of the breed, seeking to create a miniature bulldog weighing around 10 lbs./4.53 kg. Their efforts were successful enough for Toy Bulldogs to appear in competitions around 1860.

Many small breeds, including Toy Bulldogs, became the pets of choice among textile workers, who valued the companionship of the little dogs in relieving the tedium of sewing, weaving, and lace-making for hours at a time.

As something of an added benefit in a time when sanitation and pest control were far below modern standards, the small dogs kept fleas off their masters and served as superb rat catchers.

(Most people don't realize that in almost all cases, fleas prefer to live on animals, although they will bite humans if they get the chance. By nature's design, fleas are made to hide in fur, and we humans don't give them much opportunity to do so).

The living and working relationship between British textile workers and their lap dogs was disrupted by the Industrial Revolution when power looms and other machinery displaced skilled artisans. Lace makers from Nottingham, Birmingham, and Sheffield in particular, chose to migrate across the English Channel to France where the superior quality of their delicate work was still valued. Of course, they took their dogs with them.

Many of these lace workers settled in Normandy where their dogs, *les petites bouledogues*, attracted attention. Soon the animals were popular among the working class of Paris, and found themselves ensconced as shop dogs — again for their abilities as "ratters."

As French fanciers became intrigued with the breed, they did not like the exaggerated features the little dogs inherited from their larger British Bulldog antecedents. The particular traits French breeders began to refine included:

- bowed front legs
- the "roach" or dip of the spine
- heavy jowls
- pronounced underbite

The desire was for a dog with a flatter face that would have a sweeter expression, so Toy Bulldogs were crossed with Pugs and various French terrier breeds. In the process, the bulldogs regained a bit of their size, and started to pack on a more muscular appearance.

At the same time, the French fanciers deviated from the standard British Bulldog "rose" ear in favor of upright and alert ears. The look further lightened the dogs' expression and gave them a more whimsical, almost comic demeanor.

Efforts to alter the shape of the ear were augmented by British breeders who exploited the French market by selling what they considered to be undesirable Toy Bulldogs to customers across the Channel. So many dogs made the journey to France that there were soon very few examples of the breed left in England.

With continued refinement of the characteristics considered desirable by their French fans, Toy Bulldogs enjoyed a steady growth of popularity, even in some unlikely settings. Apart from being shop dogs, the animals were also adopted by Parisian prostitutes.

The ladies of the night discovered that if they had one of the appealing little bulldogs with them on a street corner, gentlemen were more likely to stop for a conversation that could become a business negotiation, if handled properly.

This mutually profitable association became so common that many of the surviving risqué postcards of the period feature not only the streetwalkers in provocative poses, but also their bulldog companions.

By this point, the animals were so distinct from their British counterparts they were routinely referred to as *le Bouledogue Français*. Consequently, the first French Bulldog Club was formed in 1880; with the first official breed registrations in 1885.

In short order, the wealthy and even royalty came to regard the dogs as a status symbol. Tsar Nicholas II of Russia and King Edward VII of England both kept Frenchies as pets. They were the pampered companions of many Left Bank writers and Impressionist painters of the period, including the flamboyant Henri de Toulouse-Lautrec as well as Edward Degas.

Wealthy Americans taking the Grand Tour of Europe began to buy and to import French Bulldogs into the United States in such numbers that the French Bull Dog Club of America was formed in 1897.

American fanciers continued to emphasize the upright ears, and were willing to pay outlandish prices for the day — as much as $3,000-$5,000 / £1,781.47 – £2,969.12 — to acquire the finest specimens for import.

By 1907, there were so many French Bulldogs in the United States that importation became unnecessary. American breeders are now given credit for perfecting the breed's erect ears and refining the overall conformation of the animals.

By the early 20th century, the little dogs achieved international status, and even began to be re-imported to Britain, although many bulldog purists continued to grouse about their perky ears.

After World War I, the French Bulldogs declined in popularity and, until the late 1980s, were considered to be somewhat rare.

Frenchies then made a rather remarkable recovery thanks to their affable personalities and willingness to adapt to urban life along with their "wash and wear" short coats.

Once again, the little charmers courted celebrities, and have been seen in the company of movie stars like Leonardo DiCaprio, Reese Witherspoon, and Nathan Lane.

French Bulldogs are so popular that they have become celebrities in their own right. Sir Charles Barkley, pictured below, has over 200,000 followers — instagram.com/barkleysircharles.

Physical Characteristics

French Bulldogs are muscular, with heavy bones, short faces, and upright "bat" ears. The round, intelligent eyes have a sweet expression under a wrinkled forehead that can give the impression that a Frenchie is a deep thinker — right before he pulls his next comical stunt.

The back has a slight dip (or fall) behind the shoulders that gradually rise to a slight peak over the loin area of the French bulldog's spine. From this rise over the loin, the back tapers downward to the onset of the tail which is naturally short. This completes the "roachback" of the breed's "topside" or "profile." If the rise begins right behind the last rib, you have a "wheelback" which is incorrect.

Brindle is the dominant standard color of the breed. Brindle is a stripy pattern of hairs which can range in color from deep copper red to pale cream or an admix of lighter hairs.

Fawns are standard, but also a recessive genetically, and range from a pale cream to a peachy hue or even into the more vivid copper and red tones.

The piebald coat color is a white coat with patches of brindle, fawn or cream; sometimes the patches are outlined by black hairs, which is the handiwork of the black-masked genetics.

Some more rare colors are created by mutations, such as merle, or by a "dilute" gene which modifies the standard colors. These are white (a piebald that is absent of color patches), a blue or blue fawn (which are diluted standard coat colors), or a black and tan (origin in this breed uncertain).

The rarer colors are discouraged by kennel clubs throughout the world since diluting coat color is connected with deafness, incurable skin disorders, and immune system disorders.

The blue coat is a disqualifying color for showing, worldwide. A flood of blues are shipped into America weekly and sold at twice the price as a dog with a legal coat color. Because some breeders are promoting "blues", it has created a volatile and controversial topic. Ethical and conservative breeders now do DNA testing to be sure their bloodline is free of this color gene.

Frenchies should weigh less than 28 lbs. / 12.7 kg in order to fit the American Kennel Club official standard, although breeders do often end up with males over this weight, meaning they cannot enter shows.

They are notorious chow hounds, given to packing on the pounds if their owners aren't careful.

Between improvement in dog food and selective breeding of healthier examples, their longevity is increasing. Their lifespan is usually 12-14 years, although I know of some who are over 18, and although normally healthy, can be prone to a number of problems, which will be discussed in full later.

French Bulldogs are a companion breed only, with no working function and are described by the American Kennel Club standard as, "well behaved, adaptable . . . active, alert, and playful, but not unduly boisterous."

Frenchies are typically social with humans and other dogs alike. They get along with well-behaved children, the disabled, and the elderly. French Bulldogs are hams at heart. They love being the center of attention, which is part of their incredible charm.

The Frenchie Personality

Although affable and adaptable, French Bulldogs do demand attention from their humans. They don't do well left alone for long periods of time and are happiest when they have the constant attention of their family or solo human.

It's common for Frenchies to be referred to as "little clowns." These dogs truly do seem to possess a sense of humor and they're never happier than when they're being loved and loving someone in return. It's hard to find a better lap dog and best canine friend than a French Bulldog.

With Children and Other Pets

The Frenchie's lovable and playful disposition makes them great companions for children who have been taught to be kind and respectful to animals. French Bulldogs are also companionable with other animals that are willing to play with them.

For cats and some older dogs that would prefer to be left alone, an enthusiastic French Bulldog can be a huge nuisance.

Some Frenchies are territorial, and may show aggression toward already established cats that have their own sense of territoriality. Make sure that all interactions are supervised until a new status quo is in place.

Barking and "Yodeling" Behavior

Although protective of their homes, French Bulldogs usually only bark when they're giving their humans an "intruder alert." Even then, a Frenchie hardly sounds vicious, but his bark is deep and fairly authoritarian. It's extremely rare for a French Bulldog to be a nuisance barker.

They can, however, let out an insistent and high-pitched "yodel" when they're unhappy or suffering from separation anxiety. It's a difficult sound to describe.

Some say it's like supercharged nails on a blackboard, others say it's the howl of an animal caught in a trap. Either way? Neither you nor the neighbors will ever forget it!

French Bulldog Breed Standard

This breed standard, accepted by the American Kennel Club is reproduced from the French Bull Dog Club of America website at frenchbulldogclub.org, with full acknowledgement of the 1991 copyright and included for purposes of reference and education only. There is no claim of authorship implied in this usage.

General Appearance

The French Bulldog has the appearance of an active, intelligent, muscular dog of heavy bone, smooth coat, compactly built, and of medium or small structure.

Expression alert, curious, and interested. Any alteration other than removal of dewclaws is considered mutilation and is a disqualification.

Proportion and Symmetry

All points are well distributed and bear good relation one to the other; no feature being in such prominence from either excess or lack of quality that the animal appears poorly proportioned.

Influence of Sex

In comparing specimens of different sex, due allowance is to be made in favor of bitches, which do not bear the characteristics of the breed to the same marked degree as do the dogs.

Size, Proportion, Substance

Weight — not to exceed 28 pounds; over 28 pounds is a disqualification.

Proportion — Distance from withers to ground in good relation to distance from withers to onset of tail, so that animal appears compact, well balanced, and in good proportion.

Substance — Muscular, heavy bone.

Head

Head large and square. Eyes dark in color, wide apart, set low down in the skull, as far from the ears as possible, round in form, of moderate size, neither sunken nor bulging. In lighter colored dogs, lighter colored eyes are acceptable. No haw and no white of the eye showing when looking forward. Ears. Known as the bat ear, broad at the base, elongated, with round top, set high on the head but not too close together, and carried erect with the orifice to the front. The leather of the ear fine and soft. Other than bat ears is a disqualification.

The top of the skull flat between the ears; the forehead is not flat but slightly rounded. The muzzle broad, deep, and well laid back; the muscles of the cheeks well developed. The stop well defined, causing a hollow groove between the eyes with heavy wrinkles forming a soft roll over the extremely short nose; nostrils broad with a well-defined line between them.

Nose black. Nose other than black is a disqualification, except in the case of the lighter colored dogs, where a lighter colored nose is acceptable but not desirable. Flews black, thick and broad, hanging over the lower jaw at the sides, meeting the underlip in front and covering the teeth, which are not seen when the mouth is closed. The underjaw is deep, square, broad, undershot, and well turned up.

Neck, Topline, Body

The neck is thick and well arched with loose skin at the throat. The back is a roach back with a slight fall close behind the shoulders; strong and short, broad at the shoulders and narrowing at the loins. The body is short and well rounded.

The chest is broad, deep, and full; well ribbed with the belly tucked up. The tail is either straight or screwed (but not curly), short, hung low, thick root, and fine tip; carried low in repose.

Forequarters

Forelegs are short, stout, straight, muscular, and set wide apart. Dewclaws may be removed. Feet are moderate in size, compact and firmly set. Toes compact, well split up, with high knuckles and short stubby nails.

Hindquarters

Hind legs are strong and muscular, longer than the forelegs, so as to elevate the loins above the shoulders. Hocks well let down. Feet are moderate in size, compact, and firmly set. Toes compact, well split up, with high knuckles and short stubby nails; hind feet slightly longer than forefeet.

Coat

Coat is moderately fine, brilliant, short, and smooth. Skin is soft and loose, especially at the head and shoulders, forming wrinkles.

Color

Acceptable colors — All brindle, fawn, white, brindle and white, and any color except those which constitute disqualification.

All colors are acceptable with the exception of solid black, mouse, liver, black and tan, black and white, and white with black, which are disqualifications. Black means black without a trace of brindle.

Gait

Correct gait is double tracking with reach and drive; the action is unrestrained, free, and vigorous.

Temperament

Well behaved, adaptable, and comfortable companions with an affectionate nature and even disposition; generally active, alert, and playful, but not unduly boisterous.

Disqualifications

Any alteration other than removal of dewclaws. Over 28 pounds in weight. Other than bat ears.

Nose other than black, except in the case of lighter colored dogs, where a lighter colored nose is acceptable.
Solid black, mouse, liver, black and tan, black and white, and white with black. Black means black without a trace of brindle.

(**Note:** To view the comparable standard for the UK-based Kennel Club, see Appendix).

Famous Bulldogs and Their Owners

No French Bulldog has ever captured Best in Show honors at either the Westminster Kennel Club Dog Show or Crufts, the world's largest dog show organized in the UK by The Kennel Club. That is not to say, however, that there have not been remarkable Frenchies in the show ring.

During the 1950s, Bouquet Nouvelle Ami took Best of Breed honors at Westminster eight years running before retiring in 1960. For the next ten years, the dog's owner, Mrs. Amanda West, continued to win Best of Breed with her other Frenchies.

In 2010, Robobull Fabelhaft I'm On Fire, a French Bulldog from Canada won the Non-Sporting Group at Westminster and was considered in the Best in Show round, losing to a Scottish Terrier, Roundtown Mercedes of Maryscot.

French Bulldogs pop up in the news from time to time. Home decorating guru, Martha Stewart, woke up her Frenchie, Francesca, and was bitten for her trouble. That same year, David and Victoria Beckham adopted a French Bulldog puppy they named Scarlet.

Singers Lady Gaga and John Legend, and actors Hugh Jackman and Jeremy Renner are Frenchie owners, and the breed has recently surfaced in movies including the 2009 movie *The Hangover* and again in 2010 in *Due Date*. On the American situation comedy *Modern Family*, the characters Jay and Gloria have a French Bulldog named Stella.

Sadly, there was also a French Bulldog aboard the ill-fated *Titanic* when it went down in 1912. The dog, Gamin de Pycombe, belonged to Robert Daniel, a 27-year-old banker who paid £150 for the animal. At today's prices, that's the equivalent of $17,000.

Manny - instagram.com/manny_the_frenchie

Most recently, a French Bulldog named Manny the Frenchie that lives in Chicago became an Internet sensation with almost half a million followers on his Instagram feed, a popular photo sharing website. He's particularly beloved for his habit of taking naps in the bathroom sink, proving that just looking at a French Bulldog can put a smile on your face!

Understand Health and Physical Challenges

Most French Bulldog owners will admit that, for them, it was love at first sight, but anyone considering this breed as a companion should pause, take a breath, and seriously think about the physical and health challenges these little dogs often face.

Frenchies are absolutely wonderful companions, but that doesn't change the fact that there are a number of issues with the breed.

Difficulty in Breeding and Birthing

While there are some French Bulldog males that can mate naturally, this is not generally the case. Typically, their legs are too short and their bodies too stocky. They simply can't reach the female, so in almost all cases, artificial insemination is required.

Also, French Bulldog puppies are more expensive in comparison to other breeds because they are typically delivered via Caesarean, due to the breed's large head and wide shoulders compared to its narrow pelvis.

Owners are advised not to attempt to breed their dogs without real expert knowledge of the health concerns and adequate funds to secure appropriate veterinary care in all phases of mating, pregnancy, and delivery.

Temperature Sensitive

The Frenchie's cute, short nose makes him highly sensitive to heat and cold. These dogs must not exert themselves in temperature extremes. They do not regulate their own body temperature well, which can prove easily fatal.

Inability to Swim

A French Bulldog should never be left unsupervised around any body of water. Even if the dog enters the water and appears to be doing well, he will go under eventually. Technically French Bulldogs can swim, but they are too heavy and not athletic enough to make it more than a few feet before they sink and cannot right themselves.

If you have a pool or want to take your Frenchie with you on outings to a lake or river, the little dog must have a life vest. There are countless tragic stories of owners that could not reach their dogs in time to save them. It is shocking how quickly a French Bulldog can drown.

Multiple Health Disorders

The breed also tends to exhibit juvenile cataracts of the eye, and premature degeneration of the vertebral discs. They are plagued with skin irritations in and around the facial wrinkles, and also experience impacted anal glands fairly frequently.

The breed snores, wheezes, and is given to excess flatulence although in fairness, this can often be as a result of poor diet and nutrition. When fed a grain-free, high quality diet, the flatulence is greatly reduced.

Popular French Bulldog Crosses

Breeding French Bulldogs is extremely difficult due to their physical conformation. Most pups are delivered by Caesarian. For this reason, there are really no recognized or sanctioned crosses.

Although you will see the following mixes advertised, and many are incredibly adorable, always have a French Bulldog cross evaluated for potential health problems before you adopt one.

Many of these crossbred dogs have much shorter lifespans and an unpredictable range of health issues.

- American French Bull Terrier (x American Pit Bull Terrier)
- American French Bulldog (x American Bulldog)
- Faux Frenchbo Bulldog (x Boston Terrier)
- French Bull Tzu (x Shih Tzu)
- French Bull Weiner (x Dachshund)
- French Bullhuahua (x Chihuahua)
- French Bulloxer (x Boxer)
- French Min (x Miniature Pinscher)

- Frenchie-Pei (Chinese Shar Pei)
- Frenchie Pug (x Pug)
- Frengle (x Beagle)
- Miniature French Bull Terrier (x Miniature Bull Terrier)
- Miniature French Schnauzer (x Miniature Schnauzer)

The appeal of any of these crosses is the notion that the resulting animal will exhibit the best traits of both breeds. This is, at best, a highly simplistic approach to genetics that rarely works out in application, especially with a dog as notoriously difficult to breed as the French Bulldog.

French Bulldog Organizations

There are many regional and local French Bulldog clubs in both the United States and the United Kingdom. The major organizations, including the major governing kennel clubs, are listed below, followed by a partial list of national clubs elsewhere in the world.

- The American Kennel Club (http://www.akc.org) was founded in 1884 to promote purebred dogs by type and function. The AKC is an advocate of canine health and wellbeing and works to protect the welfare of all dogs and to promote responsible dog ownership. It also maintains an extensive registry for the identification and verification of purebred dogs.

- The French Bull Dog Club of America (http://www.fbdca.org) was founded in 1897 and is the oldest club in the world dedicated exclusively to the breed. Members must be in good standing with the American Kennel Club and 18 years of age or older. Both individual and foreign memberships are available.

- The Kennel Club (http://www.thekennelclub.org.uk) is the largest organization in the United Kingdom dedicated to protecting and promoting the health and welfare of all dogs. It was founded in 1873 to formulate rules for the showing of dogs, the conduct of sporting field trials, and to create a registry to identify purebred animals.

- In 1902, a group of enthusiasts interested in a breed standard founded the French Bulldog Club of England (http://www.frenchbulldogclubofengland.org.uk). The group promotes the breeding of French Bulldogs according to the accepted standard and works to ensure the welfare of all Frenchies.

Other French Bull Dog Clubs and their websites include:

- Austria – http://www.frenchbulldogclubnsw.asn.au
- Australia – http://www.qldfrenchbulldogclub.com
- Canada – http://www.frenchbulldogfanciers.com
- Denmark – http://www.bulldogklubben.dk
- France – http://www.cbf-asso.org
- Germany – http://www.ikfb.de
- The Netherlands – http://www.hbc-fransebulldog.nl
- Norway – http://www.norskbulldogklubb.net
- Russia – http://frenchbulldog.ru
- Switzerland – http://www.suisse-bully.ch

Pros and Cons of French Bulldogs

French Bulldog owners are the first people to talk about the reasons to have a Frenchie, and all the reasons NOT to adopt one. This doesn't just stem from a sense of honesty, but also out of a desire to make sure these truly special dogs only go to the best homes with people who genuinely appreciate them.

Also, be warned. If you consider all of the factors, for and against having a Frenchie, and still get one? You'll probably have your own little pack in no time. These dogs are seriously addictive! People who live with French Bulldogs say there's just no other dog that will do.

Reasons to Adopt a French Bulldog

- French Bulldogs are excellent family pets. They are extremely affectionate and love to spend as much time as possible with their humans.

- They do well in small spaces, like apartments, and do not need a great deal of exercise.

- They get along well with children, as well as people who are elderly and disabled.

- Frenchies typically interact well with other pets, but prefer other animals that will play with them.

- French Bulldogs are intelligent and learn quickly (although they can be stubborn).

- They are good watchdogs, but tend to only bark when they have something to "report" to their owners.

- Low-maintenance in terms of grooming and compared to many other types of dog, odor is close to non-existent.

- Unlike English Bulldogs, Frenchies do not drool nor slobber. A few have trouble picking up kibble when eating but this is only if a mouth is wry or extremely undershot.

Reasons NOT to Adopt a French Bulldog

- These dogs are flatulent, the odor can be considerable and frequent (although this can be reduced through better diet). They also tend to belch loudly after they've eaten.

- Although Frenchies are a shorthaired breed, they can shed a great deal. Note that fawns shed more than brindles as they have a softer more plush undercoat.

- Many French Bulldogs suffer from environmental and product-based allergies.

- They are susceptible to heat stress and do not react well to severe cold.

- Most French Bulldogs can't swim.

- As breeds go, Frenchies can be incredibly stubborn.

- They are difficult dogs to housebreak.

- Many suffer from severe separation anxiety, and although they are not known to bark excessively, they can emit a very distinctive and loud "yodel."

- They may annoy other pets, especially those that are older, or cats that don't want to play with them.

- The breed is associated with a number of health issues.

Is a Frenchie the Dog for You?

Without question, French Bulldogs are adorable. For many people, it's an instant attraction, but I'm actually not a big fan of adopting a dog on the basis of "window shopping."

You need to learn everything you can about the breed — which you are clearly doing by reading this book — and preferably spend some time with Frenchies before you make your decision.

In addition to meeting with breeders and seeing their puppies, contact your local or regional kennel club, or attend a dog show. Talk to people who live with Frenchies and get their honest opinions.

Never adopt any breed until you know, in so much as it is possible to do so, what living with the dog will be like. That includes exploring all of the possible parameters of an adoption to make the right choice.

Male or Female?

The question of male versus female is raised with every breed, and even with every species. You can easily find adherents for either gender. I personally believe that the real shaping factors in any dog's personality are its early socialization and existing environment.

You will see French Bulldog enthusiasts who insist that the males are more comical and "goofy," while the females are more stubborn and determined to have their own way. To me, that characterization seems a trifle anthropomorphic, since I know many female French Bulldogs who cavort as happily and "goofily" as any of their male counterparts.

Puppy or Adult?

Adult dogs are typically adopted through a rescue group. I am a strong advocate for the work these people do, and I believe in rescue adoptions. With some breeds, however, that may only be the best choice for an experienced dog owner, not someone "meeting" the breed for the first time.

Adult dogs typically come with their own "baggage," which won't be a deal breaker for someone who knows and understands dogs. If a Frenchie has, for instance, not proven to be good with other pets, and you have no other animals, that anti-social streak can be managed.

There are, of course, advantages that go along with adopting an adult dog. You will know the animal's exact size and how well it will fit into your home, and you'll have a good idea of its exercise needs almost immediately. Older dogs also tend to be calmer and they will already be housebroken.

You do have to be careful with rescue adoptions, however. Try to determine how many homes the Frenchie has had. If the dog has just been with one other owner, you shouldn't have a problem bonding, but dogs that have been with one family after another will have difficult issues.

It's also possible to get a dog that has been extremely dependent on its former owner and is suffering from severe separation anxiety or, in the case of owner death, genuine grief. Often crate training can alleviate this type of issue by giving the dog a safe "den" when you are away.

Younger dogs, less than two years of age, adopted from shelters can have any of these problems, although they do tend to adapt fairly quickly.

Always find out if a younger dog has been given up due to a housebreaking issue. As a breed, Frenchies are difficult to train in this regard and some younger dogs are surrendered to rescue groups as a result.

Cases of severe separation anxiety that have led to various "bad" behaviors also cause many dogs to be given up. These may include barking, digging, chewing, or soiling the house. Crate training is also useful in these instances, but the help of a professional dog trainer may be necessary.

For first-time French Bulldog owners, the best option is, in my opinion, to adopt a puppy from a reputable breeder. You will not only be assured of getting a healthy pet, but you will have an expert to turn to in your first days of "parenthood," when you may well need some advice.

You and your dog will grow up together, in essence, and from an early age the Frenchie will learn your habits and routines. You will be faced with the challenges of housebreaking and other necessities of ushering a puppy into adulthood, but the reward will be a dog that knows you and your household intimately.

One or Two?

French Bulldogs are often described as one of the addictive dog breeds. People who adopt one very often wind up having more. If you have the time, space, and money to adequately care for more than one dog, there's no reason not to have two Frenchies.

Since the breed can be prone to separation anxiety, a pair of dogs can be excellent companions for one another — or they can be nervous wrecks together! It's difficult to predict, so be guided by the welfare of the dogs. Do what's best for them, not for you.

Approximate Purchase Price

Although prices can vary widely, French Bulldog puppies for sale from reputable kennels cost from $2500 to $5000 / £1500 to £3000. Even at this price there is no guarantee of getting a quality, healthy puppy. Puppy buyers still need to do their breeder homework. Show quality puppies generally start at $4500 to $7000.

The price of puppies reflects the care, attention, and costs that a reputable breeder incurs. These breeders do many health checks which will save you money in the long run. The bitch (female) has to be artificially inseminated and birth is by Caesarean section. Constant monitoring at all hours is required for the first eight weeks, with a great deal of veterinarian bills.

These websites can be good places to begin your search.

Adopt a Pet — http://www.adoptapet.com
Petango — http://www.petango.com
Pet Finder — http://www.petfinder.com

Rescue Organizations and Shelters

When you are considering rescuing a specific breed of dog or puppy, the first place to start your search will be with your local shelter and rescue groups, as well as local breeders.

You can expect to pay an adoption fee to cover the cost of spaying or neutering, which will be only a small percentage of what you would pay a breeder, and will help to support the shelter or rescue facility by defraying their costs.

French Bulldog Rescue Network
www.frenchbulldogrescue.org/

Chapter 2 – Buying a French Bulldog

For many people who have never purchased a pedigreed dog, the process can seem daunting and confusing. How do you select a breeder? How do you know if you're working with a good breeder? How do you pick a puppy? Are you paying a good price?

Pet Quality vs. Show Quality

First, you need to understand the basic terminology you will encounter to rate puppies that are offered for sale by kennels: pet quality and show quality.

Understanding the difference in these designations is often as simple as looking at the offered price. Good breeders do what they do for one reason: a desire to improve the breed.

When a puppy is not considered to be a superior example of the breed, the dog will be termed "pet quality." For most of the rest of us, even when the supposed "flaws" are pointed out, all we see is a wonderfully cute and exuberant puppy.

You will want a breeder to explain to you why the animal is considered pet quality over show quality, but since reputable breeders don't sell unhealthy dogs, this is not a deal breaker, but standard procedure.

Show quality animals can cost three times as much or more, so most of us can only afford pet quality pedigree dogs. French Bulldogs are typically reproduced via artificial insemination and it is not recommended that casual enthusiast attempt breeding, so buying a pet quality Frenchie is the norm.

Required Spaying and Neutering

When you buy a pet quality pedigree puppy it is standard for the breeder to require that the animal be spayed or neutered, typically before six months of age. The reasons for this policy are clearly tied to the primary reason for raising purebred dogs in the first place: improving the breed.

Pet quality puppies are, by their very definition, judged to be inappropriate for use in breeding programs. Also, breeders are very careful to in no way contribute to the activities of unscrupulous puppy mills.

Given the difficulty of breeding French Bulldogs, including the need for artificial insemination and delivery of puppies by Caesarian section, the requirement to spay or neuter young dogs is also a necessary safeguard of their health. If a pair successfully mated on their own, the unplanned pregnancy could easily prove fatal for the female.

Best Age to Purchase a Puppy

A French Bulldog puppy should never be removed from their mother any earlier than 8 weeks of age (at the very earliest), and leaving them until they are 10 to 16 weeks of age is preferred. This will give them the extra time they need to learn important life skills from the mother dog, including eating solid food and grooming themselves.

Also, a puppy left amongst their litter mates for a longer period of time will learn better socialization skills. Because dogs are descendants of wolves they are pack animals and prefer company, whether human beings or other dogs, to being alone. Without social contact they can become depressed and behave badly.

For the first month of a puppy's life they will be on a mother's milk-only diet. Once the puppy's teeth begin to appear, they will start to be weaned from mother's milk, and by the age of 8 weeks should be completely weaned and eating just puppy food.

How to Pick a Puppy?

My best advice is to go with the puppy that is drawn to you. My standard strategy in selecting a pup has always been to sit a little apart from a litter and let one of the dogs come to me. My late father was, in his own way, a "dog whisperer." He taught me this trick for picking puppies and it's never let me down.

I've had dogs in my life since childhood and enjoyed a special connection with them all. I will say that often the dog that comes to me isn't the one I might have chosen — but I still consistently rely on this method.

Beyond that, I suggest that you interact with your dog with a clear understanding that each one is an individual with unique traits. It is not so much a matter of learning about all French Bulldogs, but rather of learning about YOUR French Bulldog.

You will want to choose a puppy with a friendly, easy-going temperament, and your breeder should be able to help you with your selection. Also ask the breeder about the temperament and personalities of the puppy's parents and if they have socialized the puppies.

Always be certain to ask if a French Bulldog puppy you are interested in has displayed any signs of aggression or fear, because if this is happening at such an early age, you may experience behavioral troubles as the puppy becomes older.

Some people immediately turn into mush when they come face to face with cute little puppies, and still others become very emotional when choosing a puppy, which can lead to being attracted to those who display extremes in behavior.

Take a deep breath, calm yourself, and get back in touch with your common sense. Take the time to choose wisely. People who choose a dog that is not compatible with their energy and lifestyle will inevitably end up with a cascade of troubles, starting with an unhappy dog, which leads to behavioral issues, which will then lead to an unhappy family and an unhappy neighborhood.

Check Puppy Social Skills

When choosing a puppy out of a litter, look for one that is friendly and outgoing, rather than one who is overly aggressive or fearful.

Puppies who demonstrate good social skills with their litter mates are much more likely to develop into easy-going, happy adult dogs that play well with others.

Observe all the puppies together and take notice:

Which puppies are comfortable both on top and on the bottom when play fighting and wrestling with their litter mates, and which puppies seem to only like being on top?

Which puppies try to keep the toys away from the other puppies, and which puppies share?

Which puppies seem to like the company of their litter mates, and which ones seem to be loners?

Puppies that ease up or stop rough play when another puppy yelps or cries are more likely to respond appropriately when they play too roughly as adults.

Is the puppy sociable with humans? If they will not come to you, or display fear toward strangers, this could develop into a problem later in their life.

Is the puppy relaxed about being handled? If they are not, they may become difficult with adults and children during daily interactions, during grooming, or visits to the veterinarian's office.

Check Puppy's Health

Ask to see veterinarian reports to satisfy yourself that the puppy is as healthy as possible, and then once you make your decision to share your life with a particular puppy, make an appointment with your own veterinarian for a complete examination.

Before making your final pick of the litter, check for general signs of good health, including the following:

1. Breathing: will be quiet, without coughing or sneezing, and there will be no crusting or discharge around their nostrils.
2. Body: will look round and well-fed, with an obvious layer of fat over their rib cage.
3. Coat: will be soft with no dandruff or bald spots.
4. Energy: a well-rested puppy should be alert and energetic.
5. Hearing: a puppy should react if you clap your hands behind their head.
6. Genitals: no discharge visible in or around their genital or anal region.
7. Mobility: they will walk and run normally without wobbling, limping, or seeming to be stiff or sore.
8. Vision: bright, clear eyes with no crust or discharge.

How to Choose a Breeder

Since I am not an advocate of shipping live animals, and this practice is strongly discouraged with Frenchies due to their issues with temperature extremes, look for a local breeder. Talk to your vet, get in touch with your local kennel club, or attend a local or regional dog show.

Going to a dog show is my favorite method for locating breeders because it gives you the chance to see examples of the kennel's dogs. You won't be arranging an adoption at the show, but you can collect business cards and pick kennels you'd like to visit.

After you have a short list of breeders with whom you're interested in discussing a potential adoption, plan to visit every one of the kennels in person. The best facilities are those that grant visitors full access.

By really getting a good look around, you'll be able to make sure the dogs living there have enough space, that their areas are clean and free of odors, and that the animals are obviously cared for appropriately and well.

You should feel that you are part of a free exchange of information. You want a breeder who will talk about both the positives and the negatives of the breed.

What to Expect from a Good Breeder

Responsible breeders will do several things to help you pick a puppy and to make both sides in the transaction feel good about the adoption. The welfare of the dog should always be the central focus of all discussions. When you are working with a good breeder:

- You should always have the chance to see the puppy with the mother and its littermates (and if possible, the father). This is extremely important because it will give you an opportunity to judge the temperament of one or both parents, and to get a better sense of the puppy's eventual size and body conformation.

Note: Since almost all French Bulldogs are born after artificial insemination, it is likely the sire won't be resident at the kennel. In the case of this breed, seeing the mother (dam) is sufficient.

- Rather than just seeing one puppy, a good breeder will let you see and handle all the puppies.

- Breeders are responsible for registering the litter with the governing kennel club and for choosing the dog's official name. Initially each puppy will be registered in the breeder's name, so a part of the adoption process involves the transfer of the dog's registration, which requires the breeder's signature. The process of transferring the registration should be fully explained to you.

- The breeder should be able to describe to you how the puppy has been socialized and offer advice on how to continue this process after you get the dog home.

Good breeders want to know where their puppies are going and what their lives will be like with their new masters. You should be prepared to answer questions about your home and schedule, your family, and any other animals with whom you live.

Don't take this as the breeder being nosy, but rather as an excellent sign of just how much they have invested in the placement of their dogs. If a breeder does NOT ask questions along these lines, be concerned.

What the Breeder Should Provide to You

The breeder should supply all of the following to you and answer any questions you have about these items.

- You should receive a contract of sale that details the responsibilities of both parties in the adoption of the dog. The document should also explain how the puppy's registration papers will be transferred to you.

- There should be a written packet of information that offers advice on feeding, training, and exercise as well as necessary health procedures like worming and vaccinations.

- The breeder should include a pedigree of the dog's ancestry either in handwriting or an official copy from the governing kennel club.

- Make sure that you receive copies of all health records for the puppy (and parents), in particular what vaccinations the dog has received and the required schedule for booster shots. Good breeders also offer full disclosure of any potential genetic conditions associated with the breed, and are willing to discuss any testing that has been done to screen for these issues.

- You should also receive a guarantee of the puppy's health at the time of adoption, which you will likely be asked to confirm, for the safety of both parties, by taking the animal to a vet for evaluation. There should also be a detailed explanation of recompense in the event that a health condition does arise within a set period of time.

Identification Systems for Pedigree Dogs

When you adopt a pedigree dog, the animal may or may not have a means of permanent identification on its body. Systems used with pedigree dogs vary with each governing organization.

The American Kennel Club recommends permanent identification as a "common sense" practice, with the preferred methods being tattoos or microchips.

In the United Kingdom, the Kennel Club is the only organization accredited by the United Kingdom Accreditation Service to certify dog breeders through the Kennel Club Assured Breeder Scheme. Under this program, breeders are required to permanently identify their breeding stock by microchip, tattoo, or DNA profile.

Any dogs that will be traveling to or returning to the UK from another country can do so under the Pet Passport system, for which microchipping is a requirement. For more information see www.gov.uk/take-pet-abroad.

All dogs registered with the Canadian Kennel Club must be permanently identified with either a tattoo or a microchip.

Warning Signs of a Bad Breeder

- The suggestion that visiting the kennel in person isn't necessary.

- Offering to sell puppies sight unseen.

- Not being allowed to tour all parts of a kennel.

- Kennels that smell, are overly crowded, or where the animals seem nervous and apprehensive.

- Instances where you are not allowed to meet the puppies' parents.

- Unable to prove membership in any kennel club or to provide a pedigree that contains registration numbers and extends back three generations.

- Unable to produce health certification for the parents and puppies.

- Claims the health records will be sent at a later date.

- Claims there are no health problems associated with the breed. (This is absolutely NOT true with French Bulldogs).

- Tells you that the puppy has been microchipped, but does not have a scanner to prove this fact or to verify that the identification number on the chip and on the bill of sale match.

- The breeder claims it is your responsibility to take the puppy to a vet after purchase.*

- No health guarantee provided and no policy for recompense in the event a health problem does arise.

- Refusal to provide a signed bill of sale or says it will be given to you later.

* Let me clarify this point. The adoption agreement will contain a health guarantee and will require you to have the puppy

evaluated by a vet to certify that guarantee, for the protection of both parties. The puppy should, however, already have received a general check-up and initial vaccination.

Avoid Puppy Mills, Pet Shops, and Online Scams

Puppy mills exist only to churn out as many dogs as they can at minimal expense and maximum profit. The dogs are raised in substandard and often horrific conditions with no concern about their health or behavior. Inbreeding is a huge problem, leading to genetic abnormalities and shortened lifespan.

Such operations often take to the Internet and advertise their dogs as "rare" or in some way unusual. With French Bulldogs, these listings are frequently in reference to colors like blue, blue pied, blue fawn, slate, and lilac. These coats are not rare, but are a sign of bad breeding. Every one of them raises the potential for chronic and often debilitating skin conditions.

In order to help fight the proliferation of these deplorable operations, avoid pet shops! Such establishments are prime outlets for dogs raised in puppy mills. If you cannot afford a pedigreed dog, adopt from a shelter or a rescue group. These entities have the best interests of the animals at heart and are often desperately trying to place dogs that would otherwise be euthanized.

If you cannot visit the kennel in which the puppies were born, meet the parents, inspect all of the facilities, and receive complete genetic and health information on the dog, *something is wrong*.

Chapter 3 – Caring for Your New Puppy

If you have never lived with a puppy, or it has been a long time since you've shared your home with one, you may not realize or remember what a force of nature a growing dog can really be!

Their boundless energy is only outpaced by their bottomless curiosity, a combination that can spell trouble in a big way unless you take the time to puppy proof your home.

Puppy Proof Your Home in Advance

Take the attitude that you are bringing home a baby on four legs. Just as you would make sure that all the hazards have been removed from the house for an infant or toddler, do the same for your French Bulldog puppy.

I promise, he will explore every nook and cranny, and he'll try to chew on every "discovery" he unearths.

Conduct a complete inventory of all potentially poisonous household items. Look in all the cabinets and on all the shelves. Dangers easily lurk in forgotten spaces.

Move everything out of your puppy's reach and onto high shelves he's can't access, even as he gets bigger. Make sure you look for any and all cleaners and insecticides, as well as mothballs, fertilizers, and antifreeze.

A Puppy's View

As silly as it may sound, get down on the floor as close to puppy level as you can make it. For a French Bulldog puppy, you may need to lie down on your stomach and just raise your head and look around. What catches your attention?

Enticing electrical cords dangling all over the place? Drapery pulls? Loose strips of wallpaper? That old plastic bag wedged under the sofa? Don't ignore any of it. You can bet your puppy won't! Remove as many hazards as you can, and contain the ones that must remain.

Definitely put all those electrical cords and other cables in cord minders. Remember that cords and cables are both an electrocution danger and a "pull down" hazard. You'd be surprised how strong a little dog can be when he decides to pull on something — and the next thing you know, down comes the TV.

Remove items like stuffed toys, pillows, enticing knickknacks, and even prized pieces of furniture. Puppies will chew on anything! Also stow things that might *look* like a toy to an inventive Frenchie, like TV remotes, your cell phone, and your iPod or tablet computer!

Household and Garden Plants

A wide variety of household and garden plants present a toxic risk to dogs. You may have heard about the dangers of apricot and peach pits, but what about spinach and tomato vines? The American Society for the Prevention of Cruelty to Animals has created a large reference list of plants that runs to several pages.

http://www.aspca.org/pet-care/animal-poison-control/toxic-and-non-toxic-plants

I strongly recommend you go through the list and remove any plants from your home that might make your puppy sick. Remember, your new baby will chew on everything!

Bringing Your Puppy Home

Purchase an appropriate travel crate to bring your French Bulldog puppy home. A plastic crate with a fastening wire door and a carry handle is your best option. Since your puppy will be very small, you can start with a unit measuring 24" x 16.5" x 15" / 60.96 cm x 41.91 cm x 38.1 cm. That size will accommodate a dog in a weight range of 10 lbs to 20 lbs / 4.53 kg 9.07 kg. Expect to pay around $30 / £17.84.

Put a couple of puppy safe chew toys and an article of clothing you've worn recently in the crate. This will help the puppy to get to "know" you and will make the crate seem more like a "den" or safe haven. Place the puppy inside the crate and fasten the seatbelt over the crate to keep it secure on the drive home.

Make sure that the puppy has not eaten recently and has taken care of its "business" before it goes in the crate. Discuss this in advance with the kennel owner and schedule a pick-up time in between feedings. Be prepared. The little dog will whine and cry, especially if the drive is long.

If you have to drive a considerable distance, some breeders suggest mildly sedating the puppy. If you are not comfortable with this idea, take someone with you who can sit with the dog and comfort it on the way home.

Don't take more than one other person with you, however, and leave the kids at home. Having too many people in the car for the transition from kennel to new home will stress and confuse the little dog. You want the trip to be a calm, quiet, and a positive experience for your new Frenchie.

When you arrive home, let the puppy have a little time outside to relieve itself. Start reinforcing good elimination habits immediately. Praise the puppy when it goes outside. Dogs like to please their owners, so associate going outside with being a "good dog."

The Frenchie will naturally be nervous and will miss its familiar surroundings in the beginning. Try to stick to the feeding schedule used at the kennel, and use the same kind of food if possible. Put the puppy in its designated area in the house and let it explore, but make sure the dog isn't isolated and can see you.

Don't pick the puppy up every time it cries. You'll be reinforcing that behavior and the next thing you know, you'll be spending all your time holding the dog. Frenchies, no matter how young, are not above "working" their humans.

Continue to give the puppy used pieces of clothing with your scent, play a radio softly in the room, and at night put a well-wrapped warm hot water bottle in the crate.

Go Slow with the Children

If you have children, slowly introduce the puppy to them. This is not for the sake of the kids, but for the benefit of the puppy! Explain to your children, especially if they are very young, that the dog is away from its mother and the only home it has known for the first time and is scared.

Limit the amount of playtime with the puppy and how much it is handled during the first days. Emphasize quiet, gentle, "getting to know each other" time with your children. In just a matter of days, the puppy will be playing with them joyfully.

Be sure that your children know how to safely handle and carry the puppy. Monitor the first few interactions. If your child has never been around a dog and seems slightly afraid, spend time with them and help them to get to know the puppy for the safety and comfort of all concerned.

Introductions with Other Pets

Keep other pets away from your puppy for the first few days. Let the puppy smell the other pet's bedding (and vice versa) or allow sniffing under the closed bathroom door — a tried and true method of negotiating such meetings.

Carefully supervise the first face-to-face meeting. Other dogs should be on leashes and cats should be held until they are comfortable with even the sight of the new dog. Gradually extend the period of exposure and calmly separate the animals at the first sign of aggression.

Pets take their emotional cues from us. You must set the tone for first introductions. Remain calm. Don't raise your voice. Praise good behavior. Do nothing to "punish" bad behavior beyond separating the animals. Keep the meetings short and positive, without stress or trauma.

Where Will Your Frenchie Sleep?

I admit that I'm as guilty as anyone of letting my dogs sleep with me. For most breeds, that's not a problem, but you do need to consider the French Bulldog's issues with separation anxiety and that high-pitched yodel they can unleash when they're unhappy.

Crate training a puppy from an early age will provide you both with better peace of mind in the long run. A dog trained to sleep in a crate has a "den" of his own and will feel much safer and be more content when you're not at home. Also, dogs won't soil the area where they sleep, so getting in a crate routine from day one will help to facilitate housetraining.

You have two choices in crate styles, plastic portable units like those used to transport your pet to the vet, and a wire crate. Either should be large enough for the puppy to stand up, turn around, and lie down comfortably. Good ventilation is also essential. For this reason, I prefer a wire crate outfitted with comfortable padding.

You can buy an adult-sized crate for a puppy, just make sure you give the little dog a cardboard box tucked away in the back corner so he has a cozy space to snuggle into.

In addition to the crate, which you will use when you are away and at night, you can also have one or more puppy/dog beds in the home for those moments when your little Frenchie wants a nap. That's one of the funniest things about puppies. They go at full speed until they don't, and then they collapse into an adorable, snoring pile.

For a breed like the French Bulldog that should be no larger than 28 lbs. / 12.7 kg, you'll want a wire crate that is 30" x 19" x 22" / 76.2 cm x 48.26 cm x 55.88 cm, which should retail for less than $50 / £29.73. Expect to spend an additional $25 / £14.87 on a good quality crate pad.

Puppy Nutrition

Dogs require a graduated program of nutrition as they age. Puppies of four months or less should receive four small meals a day. From age four to eight months, switch to three meals per day, and then twice daily feedings at eight months and older.

French Bulldogs have a famous reputation for over-eating, which not only leads to obesity, but at this stage of life will also interfere with housetraining.

Put your puppy's food down for approximately 10-20 minutes and then take it back up again. Do not use the practice of "free feeding," which is leaving dry food out for the dog at all times.

Use only a high-quality, premium, dry, puppy food, preferably whatever the dog was used to eating at the kennel. Switching foods can lead to gastrointestinal upset, so try to maintain the dog's existing routine in so much as it is possible to do so.

Always read the label on any food you purchase to ensure that the first items listed are meat, fishmeal, or whole grains. You do not want to use a food that contains large amounts of cornmeal or meat by-products. These "filler foods" are low in nutritional value and increase the amount of waste the dog will produce per day, as well as adding to flatulence problems.

Wet foods can cause digestive issues with Frenchie puppies, and may not have the correct nutritional balance for your growing dog. Wet foods are also more difficult to measure, so the chances are much greater that the puppy will be over or under fed.

Portion control is extremely important with this breed. Measure the dry food you offer your dog and use only the recommended portion based on the puppy's weight.

Use food and water dishes that can't be tipped over. Stainless steel bowls are easier to keep clean and can be purchased as part of a unit that will slightly elevate the feeding surface. Even though your puppy may not be "tall" enough for that option just yet, he can grow into it, so you won't have to replace his dishes in the future.

Feeders with stainless steel bowls for both food and water are typically available for less than $25 / £14.87.

No Human Food!

Although it is incredibly tempting to give a French Bulldog puppy a bite of human food from the table, don't do it! If you want to give your puppy treats, buy commercially prepared treats, but never allow these "extras" to constitute more than 5% of the dog's daily food intake.

Remember that many human foods are toxic and potentially fatal to all dogs. These items include, but are not limited to:

- Chocolate
- Raisins
- Alcohol
- Human vitamins (especially those with iron)
- Mushrooms
- Onions and garlic
- Walnuts

- Macadamia nuts
- Raw fish
- Raw pork
- Raw chicken

If you allow your puppy to chew on a bone, monitor the dog closely. Use only small knuckle or joint bones. Remove the item at the first sign of splintering. Most owners prefer commercial chew toys that are rated "puppy safe."

Try to sit with your Frenchie when they eat. Don't just feed them and walk away. Many folks have come back to find a dead dog that has choked. Take a canine C.P.R. class or at least look at some You Tube videos. I happen to be certified in human CPR and have saved two of my guys from choking by using the "unconscious choking baby" method to clear their throats.

Starting Life with Your Puppy

Although your French Bulldog puppy will want to explore and "conquer" his new home, it's not a good idea to let a young dog have unsupervised run of the house, especially if he is not yet reliably housetrained.

In the beginning, plan on confining your new pet to a designated puppy "area." Baby gates are useful to create restricted areas, and are essential to keep the little dog away from obstacles, like stairs, that he may not be able to negotiate safely. Depending on the size and configuration, gates retail from $25-$100 / £14.87-£59.46.

Housebreaking

Crate training helps to housetrain your French Bulldog puppy. He will see the crate as his den and will hold his need to urinate or defecate when he is inside it. Any time you are away from the house, the dog should be in his crate, but when you return, you must immediately take the dog out to do his business.

Establish a set daily schedule and stick to it. Feed your pet the same amount of food each day at the same time and take him out afterwards. Use the same encouragements each time to get your dog to go and then praise him when he does.

Photo Credit: Kathi Liebe of Starcreek Frenchies

A feeding schedule is crucial to the housebreaking process. This will lessen the number of times the dog needs to go out, but understand that puppies have less control over their bladder and bowel movements and will need to go out after they have been especially active and have gotten excited.

On average, adult dogs go out 3-4 times a day: when they wake up, within an hour of eating, and right before bedtime. With puppies, however, don't wait more than 15 minutes after a meal.

Whether you call it house training, house breaking, or potty training, there are many different methods for helping your

French Bulldog puppy to quickly learn that their bathroom is outside rather than inside your home.

The following are methods that you may or may not have considered, all of which have their own merits, including:

- Bell training
- Exercise pen training
- Free training
- Kennel training

All of these are effective methods, so long as you add in the one critical, and often missing "wild card" ingredient, which is "human training."

When you bring home your new Frenchie puppy, they will be relying upon your guidance to teach them what they need to learn, and when it comes to house training, the first thing the human guardian needs to learn is that the puppy is not being bad when they pee or poop inside.

They are just responding to the call of Mother Nature, and you need to pay close attention right from the very beginning, because it's entirely possible to teach a puppy to go to the bathroom outside, in less than a week. Therefore, if your puppy is making bathroom "mistakes," blame yourself, not your puppy.

Check in with yourself and make sure your energy remains consistently calm and patient and that you exercise plenty of compassion and understanding while you help your new puppy learn the new bathroom rules.

French Bulldog puppies and dogs flourish with routines and happily, so do humans. Therefore, the first step is to establish a daily routine that will work efficiently for both canine and human alike.

While your puppy is still growing, on average, they can hold it approximately one hour for every month of their age. This means that if your 3-month-old puppy has been happily snoozing for two to three hours, as soon as they wake up, they will need to go outside.

Some of the first indications or signs that your puppy needs to be taken outside to relieve themselves will be when you see them:

• sniffing around
• circling
• looking for the door
• whining, crying, or barking
• acting agitated

Your happy praise will be a great help in quickly house training your puppy, because praise goes a long way toward encouraging and reinforcing future success when your French Bulldog puppy makes the right decisions.

Also, during the early stages of potty training, adding treats as an extra incentive can be a good way to reinforce how happy you are that your puppy is learning to relieve themselves in the right place. Slowly, treats can be removed and replaced with your happy praise, or you can give your puppy a treat after they are back inside.

Next, now that you have a new puppy in your life, you will want to be flexible with respect to adapting your schedule to meet their internal clocks in order to quickly teach your French Bulldog puppy their new bathroom routine.

This means not leaving your puppy alone for endless hours at a time, because firstly, they are pack animals that need companionship and your direction at all times, plus long periods alone will result in the disruption of the potty training schedule you have worked hard to establish.

If you have no choice but to leave your puppy alone for many hours, make sure that you place them in a paper-lined room or pen where they can relieve themselves without destroying your newly installed hardwood or favorite carpet.

Remember, your Frenchie is a growing puppy with a bladder and bowels that they do not yet have complete control over.

Bell Training

A very easy way to introduce your new Frenchie puppy to house training is to begin by teaching them how to ring a doorbell whenever they need to go outside.

A further benefit of training your puppy to ring a bell is that you will not have to listen to your puppy or dog whining, barking, or howling to be let out, and your door will not become scratched up from their nails.

Attach the bell to a piece of ribbon or string and hang it from a door handle or tape it to a doorsill near the door where you will be taking your puppy out when they need to relieve themselves. The string will need to be long enough so that your French Bulldog puppy can easily reach the bell with their nose or a paw.

Next, each time you take your puppy out to relieve themselves, say the word "out," and use their paw or their nose to ring the bell. Praise them for this "trick" and immediately take them outside. This type of an alert system is an easy way to eliminate accidents in the home.

Kennel Training

When you train your French Bulldog puppy to accept sleeping in their own kennel at nighttime, this will also help to accelerate their potty training, because no puppy or dog wants to relieve themselves where they sleep, which means that they will hold their bladder and bowels as long as they possibly can.

Presenting them with familiar scents by taking them to the same spot in the yard or the same street corner will help to remind and encourage them that they are outside to relieve themselves.

Use a voice cue to remind your puppy why they are outside, such as "go pee," and always remember to praise them every time they relieve themselves in the right place, so that they quickly understand what you expect of them and will learn to "go" on cue.

Exercise Pen Training

The exercise pen is a transition from kennel-only training and will be helpful for those times when you may have to leave your French Bulldog puppy for more hours than they can reasonably be expected to hold it.

Exercise pens are usually constructed of wire sections that you can put together in whatever shape you desire, and the pen needs to be large enough to hold your puppy's kennel in one half of the pen, while the other half will be lined with newspapers or pee pads.

Place your French Bulldog puppy's food and water dishes next to the kennel and leave the kennel door open (or take it off), so they can wander in and out whenever they wish, to eat or drink or go to the papers or pee pads if they need to relieve themselves.

Because they are already used to sleeping inside their kennel, they will not want to relieve themselves inside the area where they sleep. Therefore, your French Bulldog puppy will naturally go to the other half of the pen to relieve themselves on the newspapers or pee pads.

Free Training

If you would rather not confine your young Frenchie puppy to one or two rooms in your home and will be allowing them to freely range about your home anywhere they wish during the day, this is considered free training.

Never get upset or scold a puppy for having an accident inside the home, because this will result in teaching your puppy to be afraid of you and to only relieve themselves in secret places or when you're not watching.

If you catch your French Bulldog puppy making a mistake, all that is necessary is for you to calmly say "no" and quickly scoop them up and take them outside or to their indoor bathroom area.

From your puppy's point of view, yelling or screaming when they make a potty mistake is unstable energy being displayed by the person who is supposed to be their leader, and this type of behavior will only teach your puppy to fear and disrespect you.

The French Bulldog is not a difficult puppy to housebreak, and they will generally do very well when you start them off with "puppy pee pads" that you will move closer and closer to the same door that you always use when taking them outside. This way, they will quickly learn to associate going to this door when they need to relieve themselves.

Your French Bulldog puppy will always need to relieve themselves first thing in the morning, as soon as they wake up from a nap, approximately 20 minutes after they finish eating a meal, after they have finished a play session, and of course, before they go to bed at night.

NEVER punish a dog for having an accident. They cannot relate the punishment to the incident. If you catch them in the act you can say "bad dog," but don't go on and on about it. Clean up the accident using an enzymatic cleaner to eliminate the odor and return to the dog's normal routine.

Nature's Miracle Stain and Odor Removal are excellent for these kinds of incidents and is very affordable at $5 / £2.97 per 32 ounce / 0.9 liter bottle.

Also good is to go to http://www.removeurineodors.com and order yourself some "SUN" and/or "Max Enzyme," because these products contain professional-strength odor neutralizers and urine digesters that bind to and completely absorb and eliminate odors on any type of surface.

Marking Territory

Both intact male and female dogs will mark territory by urinating. This is most often an outdoor behavior, but can happen inside if a new dog is introduced to the household.

Again, use an enzymatic cleaner to remove the odor so the dog will not be attracted to use the same spot again. Since this behavior is most often seen in intact males displaying dominance, the obvious solution is to have the dog neutered.

If this is not possible, and the behavior continues, it may be necessary to separate the animals or to work with a trainer to resolve dominance issues in your little "pack."

Marking territory is not a consequence of poor housetraining and the behavior can be seen in dogs that would otherwise never go in the house.

Dealing with Separation Anxiety

Because French Bulldogs are bred to be companion dogs, they do like to be with their humans and have a real need to connect and be social. You are the center of the world for your Frenchie, so he isn't being "bad" when he misses you.

Crate training is crucial in minimizing separation anxiety, but this is not a breed that likes to be left alone for long periods of time. Whenever possible, take your dog with you, but remember that the French Bulldog is very intolerant of extremes of heat or cold. Do NOT leave your Frenchies in the car. When I say take the dog with you, I mean WITH you.

It's also a good idea to make sure that your pet has lots of other human friends. Frenchies do have a tendency to single out one human as their special person, but this is a gregarious breed. Make sure that your dog knows your friends, especially those that are willing to dog sit for a few hours or even overnight.

Set a Grooming Routine Early On

Although French Bulldogs may experience seasonal shedding, their slick coats are easy to groom and rarely require more than a weekly brushing. This will both remove loose hair and stimulate natural oils in the skin to prevent drying and flaking. Once a month you should bathe your Frenchie with mild soap and trim his nails.

I'll go into more detail on regular grooming in the next chapter, just know that this is a routine you will want to start with your puppy in the beginning and continue for life.

Common Mistakes to Avoid

Sleeping in Your Bed

Many of us humans crumble like a cheap deck of cards when we hear a crying puppy and make the mistake of allowing them to sleep with us in our bed. While this may help to calm and comfort a new puppy, it will set a dangerous precedent that can result in behavioral problems later in life. As well, a tiny French Bulldog puppy can easily be crushed by a sleeping human body.

Realize that you may not get very much sleep those first few nights and may end up sleeping on the floor beside the kennel to calm your lonely puppy.

TIP: If your bed is big enough and there is no danger of the kennel falling onto the floor in the middle of the night, you might try placing your puppy's kennel beside you on your bed until they get used to their new kennel routine.

Picking Them Up at the Wrong Time

Never pick your puppy up if they are showing fear or aggression toward an object, other dog or person, because this will be rewarding them for unbalanced behavior.

Instead, remember that your puppy is learning from watching you and "reading" your energy, therefore, how you react in every situation, and your energy level, will affect how your puppy will react.

In other words, if they are doing something you do not want them to continue, your puppy needs to be gently corrected by you, with firm and calm energy so that they learn not to react with fear or aggression.

Hand Games

Too many humans get into the habit of playing the "hand" game, where you rough up the puppy and slide them across the floor with your hands, because it's amusing for humans to see a little ball of fur scrambling to collect themselves and run back across the floor for another go.

This sort of "game" will teach your puppy to disrespect you as their leader in two different ways — first, because this "game" teaches them that humans are their play toys, and secondly, this type of "game" teaches them that humans are a source of excitement.

When your French Bulldog puppy is teething, they will naturally want to chew on everything within reach, and this will include you. As cute as you might think it is when they are young puppies, this is not an acceptable behavior and you need to gently, but firmly, discourage the habit, just like a mother dog does to her puppies when they need to be weaned.

Have compassion for your puppy during teething time, as their gums are sore and they need to chew to help relieve the pain — just make sure the pain is not being transferred to you as those milk teeth are razor sharp.

A light flick with a finger on the end of a puppy nose, combined with a firm "NO" when they are trying to bite human fingers, or any other parts of human anatomy, will discourage them from this activity. Then immediately give them something they CAN chew such as a chew toy.

If the puppy persists in chewing on you, remove yourself from the equation by getting up and walking away. If they are really feisty and persistent, put them inside their kennel with a favorite chew toy until they calm down, or take them out for a walk to burn off some of that energy.

Always praise your puppy when they stop inappropriate behavior, as this is the beginning of teaching them to understand rules and boundaries. Often we humans are quick to discipline a puppy or dog for inappropriate behavior, but we forget to praise them for their good behavior.

Treating Them Like Fur Children

Another particularly bad habit small dog owners get into is treating their French Bulldog like small fur humans.

When humans do not honor their canine companions for the amazing dogs they are, and try to turn them into small fur people, this can cause them much stress and confusion that could lead to behavioral problems.

A well-behaved French Bulldog thrives on rules and boundaries, and when they understand that there is no question you are their leader and they are your follower, they will live a contented, happy, and stress-free life.

Be sure to exert your authority, because your dog will naturally assess your personality and that of the other members of your household and try to win small challenges, which can ultimately lead to bigger problems if not controlled. If you have two dogs, they are likely to try things that they would not do if they were on their own.

Remember that dogs are a different species with different rules, for example they do not naturally cuddle and therefore they need to learn to be stroked and cuddled by humans. Therefore, be careful when approaching a dog for the first time and being overly expressive with your hands. The safest areas to touch are the back and chest — avoid patting on the head and touching the ears.

Many people will assume that a dog that is yawning is tired — this is often misinterpretation, and instead it is signaling your dog is uncomfortable and nervous about a situation.

Be careful when staring at dogs because this is one of the ways in which they threaten each other. This body language can make them feel distinctly uneasy.

Free Feeding

While free feeding a young puppy can be a good idea until they are about four or five months old, what is NOT a good idea is allowing an adult dog to continue to eat food any time they want by leaving food out for them 24/7. Remember, this is a dog, not a cat.

Free feeding can be a serious mistake, as every dog, including a French Bulldog, needs to know that their guardian is absolutely in control of their food. If your French Bulldog does not associate the food they eat with you, they may become picky eaters or think that they are the boss, which can lead to other behavioral issues later on.

Bonding with Your French Bulldog

Do not make the mistake of thinking that "bonding" with your new French Bulldog puppy or dog can only happen if you are playing or cuddling together, because the very best bonding happens when you are kindly teaching rules and boundaries, or showing them a new trick.

You will begin bonding with your Frenchie from the very first moment you bring them home from the breeder. This is the time when your puppy will be the most distraught, as they will no longer have the guidance, warmth, and comfort of their mother or their other litter-mates, and you will need to take on the role of being your new French Bulldog puppy's center of attention.

Be patient and kind with them as they are learning, because they have just been removed from all they have known and entered a totally strange, new world where they will now learn that you are their entire universe, and they must learn to safely navigate foreign surroundings.

Your daily interaction with your puppy during play sessions and especially your disciplined exercises, including going for walks on a leash, and teaching commands and tricks, will all be wonderful bonding opportunities that will bring you even closer together.

– Your Adult Dog

ur adult dog should be one of mutual enjoyment and ....ship. A French Bulldog isn't the sort of breed you'll take along for a jog, but they love short walks on days when the temperature is moderate.

Understanding your Frenchie's tolerance for exercise and play should be the foundation of your relationship with your pet.

Adult Nutrition

The same basic nutritional guidelines I discussed in Chapter 3 in regard to feeding puppies also apply to adult French Bulldogs. You always want a high-quality, premium food. I think it's actually a good idea to select a puppy food that is part of a graduated feeding program within a single product line.

Transition the dog away from the puppy food to the adult mixture, and in time, to the senior formula according to the instructions on the packaging. This ensures a consistent level of nutrition throughout the dog's life.

If you follow this strategy and select wisely for your puppy, you've set his feeding program for life. Often the breeder from whom you purchase your Frenchie will recommend a food, or your vet may have suggestions.

TIP: A great online resource is http://www.dogfoodadvisor.com. They review just about every dog food on the market and are up to date on any recalls.

Treats

Since the creation of the first dog treat over 150 years ago, the myriad of choices available on every pet store, feed store, and grocery store shelf almost outnumbers those looking forward to eating them.

Today's treats are not just for making us guilty humans feel better because we've left our dog home alone for hours, or because it makes us happy to give our pets something they really like, today's treats are designed to improve our dog's health.

Some of us humans treat our dogs just because, others use treats for training purposes, others for health, while still others treat for a combination of reasons.

Whatever reason you choose to give treats to your French Bulldog, keep in mind that if we treat our dogs too often throughout the day, we may create a picky eater who will no longer want to eat their regular meals.

As well, if the treats we are giving are high calorie, we may be putting our dog's health in jeopardy by allowing them to become overweight.

Generally, the treats you feed should not make up more than approximately 10% of their daily food intake.

Rawhide goes through an extensive processing with unhealthy chemicals, the result of which is that the rawhide is no longer food and, as such, no longer has to comply with food or health regulations. Ingested rawhide can swell to four times its size, causing mild to severe gastric blockages that require surgery.

Pigs Ears are extremely high in fat and processed with unhealthy chemicals that can cause stomach upset, vomiting, and diarrhea.

Hoof Treats include cow, horse, and pig hooves that are processed with preservatives, including insecticides, lead, bleach, arsenic-based products, and antibiotics to kill bacteria. If all the bacteria are not removed, your dog could also suffer from Salmonella poisoning. These can also cause chipping or breaking of your dog's teeth, as well as blockages in your dog's intestines.

Hard Treats: There are so many choices of hard or crunchy treats available that come in many varieties of shapes, sizes, and flavors, that you may have a difficult time choosing. If your French Bulldog will eat them, hard treats will help to keep their teeth cleaner.

Whatever you choose, read the labels and make sure that the ingredients are high quality and appropriately sized for your French Bulldog friend. Also ... check any treats to see the country of origin. I would be highly suspect of anything from China as there have been issues including deaths from "chicken breast jerky" from China. The large pet store chains in the U.S. have decided to stop carrying many of the Chinese treats.

Soft Treats are also available in a wide variety of flavors, shapes, and sizes for all the different needs of our fur friends and are often used for training purposes as they have a stronger smell.

Often smaller dogs, such as the French Bulldog, prefer the soft, chewy treats over the hard, crunchy ones.

Dental Treats or chews are designed with the specific purpose of helping your French Bulldog to maintain healthy teeth and gums. They usually require intensive chewing and are often shaped with high ridges and bumps to exercise the jaw and massage gums while removing plaque build-up near the gum line.

Freeze-dried and Jerky Treats offer a tasty morsel most dogs find irresistible, as they are usually made of simple, meaty ingredients, such as liver, poultry, and seafood. These treats are usually light weight and easy to carry around, which means they can also be great as training treats or to take with you when you and your dog go on a long walk.

Human Food Treats often contain additives and ingredients that are toxic or poisonous to our fur friends, so be very careful when sharing human food as treats for your French Bulldog. Choose simple, fresh foods with minimal or no processing, such as lean meat, poultry, or seafood.

Even today, far too many dog food choices continue to have far more to do with being convenient for us humans to serve than they do with being a well-balanced, healthy food choice for a canine.

Sadly, because dogs will eat pretty much anything, we humans have been guilty of feeding pretty much anything to them for a very long time.

In order to choose the right food for your French Bulldog, first it's important to understand a little bit about canine physiology and what Mother Nature intended when she created our furry companions. Perhaps most important when choosing an appropriate diet for our dogs is taking a closer look at our dog's teeth, jaws, and digestive tract.

While humans are omnivores who can derive energy from eating plants, our canine companions are carnivores, which means they derive their energy and nutrient requirements from eating a diet consisting mainly or exclusively of the flesh of animals, birds, or fish.

The Canine Teeth and Jaw

The first part of your dog you will want to take a good look at when considering what to feed them will be their teeth.

Unlike humans, who are equipped with wide, flat molars for grinding grains, vegetables, and other plant-based materials, canine teeth are all pointed because they are designed to rip, shred, and tear into meat and bone.

Another obvious consideration when choosing an appropriate food source for our fur friends is the fact that every canine is born equipped with powerful jaws and neck muscles for the specific purpose of being able to pull down and tear apart their hunted prey.

The structure of the jaw of every canine is such that it opens widely to hold large pieces of meat and bone, while the mechanics of a dog's jaw permits only vertical (up and down) movement that is designed for crushing.

The Canine Digestive Tract

A dog's digestive tract is short and simple and designed to move their natural choice of food (hide, meat, and bone) quickly through their systems.

The canine digestive system is simply unable to properly break down vegetable matter, which is why whole vegetables look pretty much the same going into your dog as they do coming out the other end.

Given the choice, most dogs would never choose to eat plants and grains, or vegetables and fruits over meat, however, we humans continue to feed them a kibble-based diet that contains high amounts of vegetables, fruits, and grains with low amounts of meat.

Part of this is because we've been taught that it's a healthy, balanced diet for humans, and therefore, we believe that it must be the same for our dogs, and part of this is because all the fillers that make up our dog's food are less expensive and easier to process than meat.

How much healthier and long lived might our beloved French Bulldog be if, instead of largely ignoring nature's design for our canine companions, we chose to feed them whole, unprocessed, species-appropriate food with the main ingredient being meat?

Whatever you decide to feed your dog, keep in mind that just as too much wheat, other grains, and other fillers in our human diet is having a detrimental effect on our health, the same can be very true for our best fur friends.

Our dogs are also suffering from many of the same life-threatening diseases that are rampant in our human society as a direct result of consuming a diet high in genetically altered, impure, processed, and packaged foods.

What is the Best Food?

The dog food industry is very big business, and because there are now almost limitless choices, there is much confusion and endless debate when it comes to answering the question, "What is the best food for my dog?"

Educating yourself by talking to experts and reading everything you can find on the subject, plus taking into consideration several relevant factors, will help to answer the dog food question.

For instance, where you live may dictate what sorts of foods you have access to. Other factors to consider will include the particular requirements of your dog, such as their age, energy, and activity levels.

Next will be expense, time, and quality. While we all want to give our dogs the best food possible, many humans lead very busy lives and cannot, for instance, prepare their own dog food, but still want to feed a high quality diet that fits within their budget.

The BARF Diet

While some of us believe we are killing ourselves as well as our dogs with processed foods, others believe that there are dangers in feeding raw foods.

Raw feeding advocates believe that the ideal diet for their dog is one that would be very similar to what a dog living in the wild would have access to, and these canine guardians are often opposed to feeding their dog any sort of commercially manufactured pet foods.

On the other hand, those opposed to feeding their dogs a raw or Biologically Appropriate Raw Food (BARF) diet believe that the risks associated with food-borne illnesses during the handling and feeding of raw meats outweigh the purported benefits.

Interestingly, even though the United States Food and Drug Administration (FDA) states that they do not advocate a raw diet for dogs, they do advise that for those who wish to take this route, following basic hygiene guidelines for handling raw meat can minimize any associated risks.

Further, high pressure pasteurization (HPP), which is high pressure, water-based technology for killing bacteria, is USDA approved for use on organic and natural food products and is being utilized by many commercial raw pet food manufacturers.

Raw meats purchased at your local grocery store contain a much higher level of acceptable bacteria than raw food produced for dogs, because the meat purchased for human consumption is meant to be cooked, which will kill any bacteria that might be present.

This means that canine guardians feeding their dogs a raw food diet can be quite certain that commercially prepared raw foods sold in pet stores will be safer than raw meats purchased in grocery stores.

Many guardians of high energy, working breed dogs will agree that their dogs thrive on a raw or BARF diet and strongly believe that the potential benefits of feeding a dog a raw food diet are many, including:

- Healthy, shiny coats
- Decreased shedding
- Fewer allergy problems
- Healthier skin
- Cleaner teeth
- Fresher breath
- Higher energy levels
- Improved digestion
- Smaller stools
- Strengthened immune system
- Increased mobility in arthritic pets
- General increase or improvement in overall health

All dogs, whether working breed or lap dogs, are amazing athletes in their own right, therefore every dog deserves to be fed the best food available.

A raw diet is a direct evolution of what dogs ate before they became our domesticated pets and we turned toward commercially prepared, easy-to-serve dry dog food that required no special storage or preparation.

The Dehydrated Diet

Dehydrated dog food comes in both raw and cooked forms, and these foods are usually air-dried to reduce moisture to the level where bacterial growth is inhibited.

The appearance of dehydrated dog food is very similar to dry kibble, and the typical feeding methods include adding warm water before serving, which makes this type of diet both healthy for our dogs and convenient for us to serve.

Dehydrated recipes are made from minimally processed fresh whole foods to create a healthy and nutritionally balanced meal that will meet or exceed the dietary requirements for healthy canines.

Dehydrating removes only the moisture from the fresh ingredients, which usually means that because the food has not already been cooked at a high temperature, more of the overall nutrition is retained.

A dehydrated diet is a convenient way to feed your dog a nutritious diet, because all you have to do is add warm water and wait five minutes while the food re-hydrates so your French Bulldog can enjoy a warm meal.

The Kibble Diet

While many canine guardians are starting to take a closer look at the food choices they are making for their furry companions, there is no mistaking that the convenience and relative economy of dry dog food kibble, which had its beginnings in the 1940s, continues to be the most popular pet food choice for most humans.

While feeding a high-quality, bagged kibble diet that has been flavored to appeal to dogs and supplemented with vegetables and fruits to appeal to humans may keep most every French Bulldog companion happy and healthy, you will need to decide whether this is the best diet for them.

Exercise, Walks, and Play

French Bulldogs are very prone to heat stroke, so you must never expose your pet to high temperatures. This is a breed that will enjoy a brisk walk in the cool of the morning followed by a nice long nap.

Photo Credit: Kathi Liebe of Starcreek Frenchies

Also, Frenchies do not swim well. They are too heavy and can easily drown if left unattended near the water. Even if your dog seems to enjoy splashing in the shallows, consider all bodies of water as a danger and stay with your dog at all times. You might want to consider investing in a canine life vest if you spend a lot of time beside the pool or at a lake or river with your pet.

Life jackets for dogs in the Frenchie weight range are typically sized as either small or medium and are available for $20 to $25 / £11.88 to £14.85. Always take your dog with you to the store to fit the item, or bring both sizes home so you can return the one that doesn't work.

Limit all periods of playtime with your French Bulldogs to 15 minutes or less, followed by calm, cuddling downtime, which Frenchies LOVE, and confine your pet's daily walk to the coolest period of the day in your region.

Remember, however, that Frenchies are also intolerant of extreme cold, so in the winter, outfit your pet with a coat or sweater and on the coldest days, play with him indoors rather than attempting a walk.

Collar or Harness?

I find many vets tell owners to use harnesses. I don't, although I had a dog that was hard to lead break and used one for a short time.

I believe, during training, that one should keep the dog's tendency to be impulsive and fearless in front of your mind. I use a Martingale Resco with a pup on a short lead and use a "tug and release" technique to keep the dog in control.

I train pups on a short lead, a bit slack around the throat. After a pup is solid in regard to obeying me, I give it more slack and then use the retractable type lead for casual walks. In the showring, I gait them on a free lead too.

I don't agree with the idea of a halter, although I don't interfere when vets tell clients to use a halter with this breed. My idea is to give the pup little freedom until it can be trusted and is under control. I also encourage buyers to go to puppy classes.

Standard Leash or Retractable?

For the most part, the decision to buy a standard, fixed length leash or a retractable lead is up to you. Do bear in mind that some facilities like groomers, vet clinics, and dog daycares ask that you not bring your animal in on a retractable lead as the long line represents a trip and fall hazard for other human clients.

Fixed length leashes can cost as little as $5 / £2.97, while retractable leads are typically less than $15 / £8.91.

Regardless of the kind of lead you choose, your dog will have to get used to responding to your control of the leash.

Never jerk on the lead or "drag" the dog with it. If your dog sits down and refuses to move, walk over and pick him up. Never let a French Bulldog have his way or he'll be walking you!

It won't be long before your Frenchie associates the lead with positive outings and adventures with you. Don't be surprised if your dog picks the leash up and brings it to you, which is a pretty clear message, "Let's go!"

Some Tips on Walking Your Dog

Because walks and going out are things that dogs enjoy, and because your pet will want to please you, you can instill some good behaviors on command around the whole process. Teach your dog the "sit" command by using the word and making a downward pointing motion with your finger or the palm of your hand.

Reward the dog with a treat each time he performs correctly. Then pair the sit command with the pleasure of a walk by refusing to attach the lead to the harness until your pet sits. Make attaching the leash and saying, "Okay, let's go!" be the reward.

Any time the dog tries to pull you or jerk at the leash, stop the walk, pick up the dog, and start over with the sit command. Praise and reward the dog for walking properly at the end of the lead and for stopping when you stop. The more than you can reinforce the walk as a shared activity, the quieter and more calm your dog will be.

Your dog's main sense is scent, which is why when you take them for a walk they spend a lot of time sniffing everything. They gather an amazing amount of information such as being able to determine which dogs were recently in the area, their gender, their current health, and age. Incredible!

When two dogs meet they are likely to go up to each other and sniff near each other's jaw and then around the rear-end area.

Have you ever visited a friend and their dog has come up to you and sniffed your groin area? This may have caused some embarrassment but this is simply a dog's way of learning about you by picking up scents.

Establishing Basic Commands

By their nature, dogs are pack animals. You want to delineate yourself as the leader of their pack. Using consistent vocabulary and establishing basic commands is always a good idea.

On a whole, French Bulldogs do not bark often unless they have something they want to tell you like, "Hey! That big brown truck with UPS on the side just pulled up in the driveway again!" If your dog does exhibit barking at an inappropriate time, use the command, "Quiet," followed by "bad dog."

Do the same thing when your Frenchie picks something up you don't want him to have, but use the phrase, "Drop it!" or "Leave it!" For jumping-up behavior, use "Down!" By staying consistent and speaking firmly, you reinforce your authority as the leader of the pack and cater to your pet's natural desire to please.

These and other basic commands like "sit" and "stay" are relatively easy to convey to a breed as intelligent and loyal as a Frenchie.

Photo Credit: Kathi Liebe of Starcreek Frenchies

Generally speaking, the French Bulldog will be easy to train so long as their guardian is gentle and patient, because using harsh or loud training methods will frighten a French Bulldog and cause them to shut down.

All training sessions should be happy and fun-filled, with plenty of rewards and positive reinforcement, which will ensure that your French Bulldog is an excellent student who looks forward to learning new commands and tricks.

Dog Whispering or Dog Training?

Many people can be confused when they need professional help with their dog, because for many years, if you needed help with your dog, you contacted a "dog trainer" or took your dog to "puppy classes" where your dog would learn how to sit or stay.

The difference between a dog trainer and a dog whisperer would be that a "dog trainer" teaches a dog how to perform certain tasks, and a "dog whisperer" alleviates behavior problems by teaching humans what they need to do to keep their particular dog happy.

Often, depending on how soon the guardian has sought help, this can mean that the dog in question has developed some pretty serious issues, such as aggressive barking, lunging, biting or attacking other dogs, pets, or people.

Dog whispering is often an emotional roller coaster ride for the humans involved that unveils many truths when they finally realize that it has been their actions (or inactions) that have likely caused the unbalanced behavior that their dog is now displaying.

Once solutions are provided, the relief for both dog and human can be quite palpable and cathartic when they realize that with the correct direction, they can indeed live a happy life with their dog.

All specific methods of training, such as "clicker training," fall outside of what every dog needs to be happy, because training your dog to respond to a clicker, which you can easily do on your own, and then letting them sleep in your bed, eat from your plate, and any other multitude of things humans allow, are what makes the dog unbalanced and causes behavior problems.

I always say to people, don't wait until you have a severe problem before getting some dog whispering or professional help of some sort, because "With the proper training, Man can learn to be dog's best friend."

Puppy Training

Puppy training can begin as soon as you bring your French Bulldog puppy home from the breeder.

Most humans believe that they need to take their puppy to puppy classes, and generally speaking, this is a good idea for any young French Bulldog (after they have had their vaccinations), because it will help to get them socialized.

"Come," "Sit," and "Stay" will be the three most important words you will ever teach your French Bulldog puppy.

These three basic commands will ensure that your French Bulldog remains safe in almost every circumstance.

For instance, when your puppy correctly learns the "Come" command, you can always quickly bring them back to your side should danger approach.

When you teach your French Bulldog puppy the "Sit" and "Stay" commands, you will be further establishing your leadership role. A puppy who understands that their human guardian is their leader will be a safe and happy follower.

Choosing a Discipline Sound

Choosing a "discipline sound" that is the same for every human family member will make it much easier for your puppy to learn what they can or cannot do.

The best types of sounds are short and sharp. It doesn't really matter what the sound is, so long as everyone in the family agrees to use the same sound. A sound that is very effective for most puppies and dogs is a simple "UH" sound said sharply and with emphasis.

Most puppies and dogs respond immediately to this sound and, if caught in the middle of doing something they are not supposed to be doing, they will quickly stop and give you their attention or back away from what they were doing.

Beginner Leash Lesson

You need a 4 or 6-foot leash and a properly sized Martingale training collar that fits your puppy.

TIP: During early leash lessons, you can also put your French Bulldog puppy in a harness and clip an extra leash onto the harness, so that you can easily lift them over cigarette butts or other enticing pieces of garbage they may want to put in their mouth.

The most important bonding exercise you will experience with your new French Bulldog puppy is when you go out for your daily walks together.

Far too many humans get lazy or impatient at this early and very impressionable time in a puppy's life and simply ignore the importance of this critical training time. It is not only important for your puppy's exercise, but also establishes you as their leader.

Too many guardians of small puppies simply pick up their puppy and carry them outside to relieve themselves, because they are too impatient to wait for the puppy to understand how the collar and leash work.

Carrying a puppy does not help them learn the routine that will be required of them once they become adults and can also create an unstable relationship between the guardian and the French Bulldog puppy.

Even though a French Bulldog is able to self-exercise to some degree when spending a lot of their time indoors, always exercising inside will not help to fulfill their natural roaming urges, because every dog instinctually needs to roam their territory.

When you take your new French Bulldog puppy outside for walks on a leash every day, you will be engaging them in valuable multi-tasking training, including:

• The discipline of following their leader.
• Learning to walk on leash.
• Expanding their knowledge of different smells.
• Exercising both their body and their mind.
• Gently growing and developing bones and muscles.
• Socialization with other humans and animals.
• Experience of different environments.
• Trust and respect of their guardian.

As soon as you bring your new puppy home, you will want to teach them how to walk at your side while on a leash without pulling.

Thankfully, when you bring your new puppy home, you will have many opportunities for leash training in combination with potty training, because every time your puppy needs to go out to relieve themselves, you can slip on their Martingale training collar and snap on that leash.

During your first on-leash walk, your French Bulldog puppy may struggle or fight against having a collar around their neck, because the sensation will be new to them. However, at the same time they will want to go with you, so exercise patience and encourage them to walk with you.

Be careful never to drag them, and if they pull backward and refuse to walk forward with you, simply stop for a moment, while keeping slight forward tension on the leash until your French Bulldog puppy gives up and moves forward.

Immediately reward them with your happy praise, and if they have a favorite treat, this can be an added incentive when teaching them to walk on their leash.

Photo Credit: Bev Anderson of Timepieces French Bulldogs Perm Reg'd

Always walk your puppy on your left side with the leash slack so that they learn that walking with you is a relaxing experience. Keep the leash short enough so that they do not have enough slack to get in front of you.

If they begin to create tension in the leash by pulling forward or to the side, simply stop moving, get them back beside you and start over.

Be patient and consistent with your puppy and very soon they will understand exactly where their walking position is and will walk easily beside you without any pulling or leash tension.

Remember that walking with a new puppy is an exciting experience for them, as they will want to sniff everything and explore their new world, so give them lots of understanding and don't expect them to be perfect.

The Stubborn Adolescent

The adolescent period in a young French Bulldog's life, between the ages of 6 and 12 months, is the transitional stage of both physical and psychological development when they are physically almost full grown in size, yet their minds are still developing, and they are testing their boundaries and the limits that their human companions will endure.

This can be a dangerous time in a puppy's life, because this is when they start to make decisions on their own, which can lead to developing unwanted behaviors.

Learning how to make decisions on their own would be perfectly normal and desirable if your French Bulldog puppy was living in the wild, amongst a pack of dogs, because it would be necessary for their survival.

However, when living within a human environment, your puppy must always adhere to human rules, and it will be up to their human guardians to continue their vigilant, watchful guidance in order to make sure that they do.

Many humans are lulled into a false sense of security when their new French Bulldog puppy reaches the age of approximately six months, because the puppy has been well socialized and long since been house trained.

The real truth is that the serious work is only now beginning, and the humans and their new French Bulldog puppy could be in for a time of testing that could seriously challenge the relationship and leave the humans wondering if they made the right decision. The trust and respect that has been previously built can be damaged, sometimes irreparably.

While not all puppies will experience a noticeable adolescent period of craziness, most young dogs do commonly exhibit at least some of the usual adolescent behaviors, including reverting to previous puppy behaviors.

Some of these adolescent behaviors might include destructive chewing of objects they have previously shown no interest in, selective hearing or ignoring previously learned commands, displaying aggressive behavior, jumping on everyone, barking at everything that moves, or even reverting to relieving themselves in the house, even though they were house trained months ago.

Keeping your cool and recognizing these adolescent signs are the first step toward helping to make this transition period easier on your puppy and all family members.

The first step to take that can help keep raging hormones at bay is to spay or neuter your French Bulldog puppy just prior to the onset of adolescence, at around five or six months of age. While spaying or neutering a French Bulldog puppy will not eliminate the adolescent phase, it will certainly help.

Once your French Bulldog puppy has been spayed or neutered, you will want to become more active with your young dog, both mentally and physically, by providing them with continued and more complex, disciplined exercises.

This can be accomplished by enrolling your adolescent French Bulldog in a dog whispering session to make sure that necessary rules and boundaries are in place, or a more advanced obedience class that will help them to continue their socialization skills, while also developing their brain.

When your French Bulldog is provided with sufficient daily exercise and continued socialization that provides interest and expands their mind, they will be able to transition through the adolescent stage of their life much more seamlessly.

Yelling Makes it Worse

If your French Bulldog puppy happens to be especially unruly during their adolescent phase, you will need to simply limit their opportunities for making mistakes.

It does absolutely no good to yell at your French Bulldog puppy for engaging in behavior you are not happy with, and in fact, yelling will only desensitize your young dog from listening to any of your commands.

Further, although you may eventually get the results you want, if you yell loud enough, your puppy will then be reacting out of fear, rather than respect, and this is not the type of relationship you want to have.

Displaying calm, yet assertive, energy is the ONLY energy that will help your adolescent puppy understand what is required of them.

All other human emotions are "read" by puppies and dogs as being unstable, and not only will they not understand you, they will not respect you for displaying confusing energies.

Make sure that your French Bulldog is within eyesight at all times, so that if they do find an opportunity to make a mistake, you can quickly show them what is permitted and what is not.

Keeping on top of house training is also a good idea during the adolescent period of your puppy's life, because some adolescent puppies may forget that they are already house trained.

This means actually taking the time to be involved in the process by leashing up your French Bulldog and physically taking them outside whenever they need to relieve themselves.

This sort of a routine is also a disciplined exercise that will help to reinforce in your puppy's mind that you are the boss.

Rewarding Unwanted Behavior

It is very important to recognize that any attention paid to an out-of-control, adolescent puppy, even negative attention, is likely to be exciting and rewarding for your Frenchie puppy.

Chasing after a puppy when they have taken something they shouldn't have, picking them up when barking or showing aggression, pushing them off when they jump on other people, or yelling when they refuse to come when called, are all forms of attention that can actually be rewarding for most puppies.

It will be your responsibility to provide structure for your puppy, which will include finding acceptable and safe ways to allow your puppy to vent their energy without being destructive or harmful to others.

Basic First Commands

All that's necessary for effectively teaching or reinforcing your puppy's basic first commands is a calm, consistent approach, combined with endless patience.

Most puppies are ready to begin simple training at about 10 to 12 weeks of age, however, be careful not to overdo it when they are under six months of age, as their attention span will be short and they will tire easily.

Make training sessions positive and fun and no more than 5 or 10 minutes, with lots of praise and/or treats so that your puppy will be eagerly looking forward to their next session.

Also, introduce the hand signals that go along with the verbal commands so that once they learn both, you can remove the verbal commands and only use hand signals.

Photo Credit: Richard & Michelle Shannon of Smokey Valley Kennel

Basic Hand Signals

Hand signal training is by far the most useful and efficient training method for every dog, including the French Bulldog.

This is because all too often we inundate our canine companions with a great deal of chatter and noise that they really do not understand, because English is not their first language.

Contrary to what some humans might think, the first language of a French Bulldog, or any dog, is a combination of sensing energy and watching body language, which requires no spoken word or sound.

Therefore, when we humans take the time to teach our dog hand signals for all their basic commands, we are communicating with them at a level they instinctively understand, plus we are helping them to become focused and attentive followers, as they must watch us to understand what is required of them.

Come

While most puppies are capable of learning commands and tricks at a surprisingly young age, the first and most important command you need to teach your puppy is the recall or "Come" command.

The hand signal for "Come" is your arms spread wide open. This is a command they can see from a great distance. Always show the hand signal for the command at the same time you say the word.

Begin the "Come" command inside your home. Go into a larger room, such as your living room area. Place your puppy in front of you and attach their leash or a longer line to their collar while you back away from them a few feet.

Say the command "Come" in an excited voice and hold your arms open wide. If they do not immediately come to you, gently give a tug on the leash so that they understand that they are supposed to move toward you. When they come to you praise them and give a treat they really enjoy.

Once your puppy can accomplish a "Come" command almost every time inside your home, you can then graduate them to a nearby park or quiet outside area where you will repeat the process.

You may want to purchase an extra-long line (25 or 50 feet) so that you are always attached to your French Bulldog puppy and can encourage them in the right direction should they become distracted.

At your leisure, firmly ask them to "Come" and show the hand signal. If they do not immediately come to you, give a firm tug with the lunge line so that they understand what you are asking of them.

If they still do not "Come" toward you, simply reel them in until they are in front of you, praise them and give a treat. Then let them wander about again, until you are ready to ask them to "Come."

Sit

The "Sit" and "Stay" commands are both easy commands to teach, and in combination with the "Come" command, will help to keep your French Bulldog puppy safe and out of danger in most every circumstance. Find a quiet time to teach these commands when your puppy is not tired.

Every time you take your French Bulldog out for a walk, get in the habit of asking them to sit while you put on their leash — then ask them to sit again and wait while you put on your shoes.

Most dogs will sit when you ask them while you put on their leash, and as soon as the leash is on, and you are busy putting on your coat or shoes, they get excited and stand up; ask them to sit again and calmly wait while you are getting yourself ready.

Ask your puppy to "Sit," and if they do not yet understand the command, hold a treat over their head, which can cause them to automatically sit, or show them what you mean by gently squeezing with your thumb and middle finger the area across the back that joins with their back legs.

Do not just push or force them down into a sit, as this can cause damage to their back or joints. When they sit, give them a treat and praise them.

When you say the word "Sit," at the same time, show them the hand signal for this command, which is bending your arm at the elbow and raising your right hand, palm open facing upward, toward your shoulder.

Slowly remove the treats as reward and replace the treat with a "life reward," such as a chest rub or a thumbs-up signal.

Stay

Once your French Bulldog puppy can reliably "Sit," say the word "Stay" and hold your outstretched arm palm open toward their head and back away a few steps.

If they try to follow, calmly say "No" and put them back into "Sit." Give a treat and then say again, "Stay," with the hand signal and back away a few steps. Continue to practice this until your dog understands that you want them to stay sitting and not move toward you.

With all commands, when your French Bulldog is just learning, be patient and always reward them with a treat and your happy praise for a job well done.

TIP: Use your dominant hand for the "Stay" command and you will have better results, because the strongest energy emanates from the palm of your dominant hand. For instance, if you are right handed, use your right hand.

Once your puppy is sitting and staying, you can then ask them to "Come." Don't forget to use the open arms hand signal for "Come."

I would encourage you to be extra excited when training the "Come" command, so that your puppy will always enjoy correctly responding and immediately come running to you, because they know they will receive a tasty treat, your happy praise, or both.

Otherwise, the only time you will show some excitement is when you are praising a command well executed.

You do not want your puppy to get the idea that humans are a source of excitement, because this can lead to many other problems in later life.

Practice these three basic commands everywhere you go, and pretty soon you will have an automatically sitting puppy who impresses all your neighbors, because they sit whenever you stop moving without you saying the command or giving the signal.

First Tricks

When teaching your French Bulldog their first tricks, in order to give them extra incentive, find a small treat that they would do anything to get, and give the treat as rewards to help solidify a good performance.

Most dogs will be extra attentive during training sessions when they know that they will be rewarded with their favorite treats.

If your French Bulldog is less than six months old when you begin teaching them tricks, keep your training sessions short (no more than 5 or 10 minutes) and make the sessions lots of fun.

As your French Bulldog becomes an adult, you can extend your sessions because they will be able to maintain their focus for longer periods of time.

Shake a Paw

Who doesn't love a dog who knows how to shake a paw? This is one of the easiest tricks to teach your Frenchie.

TIP: Most dogs are naturally either right or left pawed. If you know which paw your dog favors, ask them to shake this paw.

Find a quiet place to practice, without noisy distractions or other pets, and stand or sit in front of your dog. Place them in the sitting position and hold a treat in your left hand.

Say the command "Shake" while putting your right hand behind their left or right paw and pulling the paw gently toward yourself until you are holding their paw in your hand. Immediately praise them and give them the treat.

Most dogs will learn the "Shake" trick very quickly, and in no time at all, once you put out your hand, your French Bulldog will immediately lift their paw and put it into your hand, without your assistance or any verbal cue.

Practice every day until they are 100% reliable with this trick, and then it will be time to add another trick to their repertoire.

Roll Over

You will find that just like your French Bulldog is naturally either right or left pawed, that they will also naturally want to roll either to the right or the left side. Take advantage of this by asking your dog to roll to the side they naturally prefer.

Sit with your dog on the floor and put them in a lie down position. Hold a treat in your hand and place it close to their nose without allowing them to grab it, and while they are in the lying position, move the treat to the right or left side of their head so that they have to roll over to get to it.

You will quickly see which side they want to naturally roll to, once you see this, move the treat to that side. Once they roll over to that side, immediately give them the treat and praise them.

You can say the verbal cue "Over" while you demonstrate the hand signal motion (moving your right hand in a half circular motion) from one side of their head to the other.

Sit Pretty

While this trick is a little more complicated, and most dogs pick up on it very quickly, remember that this trick requires balance, and every dog is different, so always exercise patience.

Find a quiet space with few distractions and sit or stand in front of your dog and ask them to "Sit."

Have a treat nearby (on a countertop or table) and when they sit, use both of your hands to lift up their front paws into the sitting pretty position, while saying the command "Sit Pretty." Help them balance in this position while you praise them and give them the treat.

Once your French Bulldog can do the balancing part of the trick quite easily without your help, sit or stand in front of your dog while asking them to "Sit Pretty" and hold the treat above their head, at the level their nose would be when they sit pretty.

If they attempt to stand on their back legs to get the treat, you may be holding the treat too high, which will encourage them to stand up on their back legs to reach it. Go back to the first step and put them back into the "Sit" position and again lift their paws while their backside remains on the floor.

The hand signal for "Sit Pretty" is a straight arm held over your dog's head with a closed fist.

Make this a fun and entertaining time for your French Bulldog and practice a few times every day until they can "Sit Pretty" on hand signal command every time you ask.

TIP: Place your French Bulldog beside a wall when first teaching this trick so that they can use the wall to help their balance.

A young French Bulldog puppy should be able to easily learn these basic tricks before they are six months old, and when you are patient and make your training sessions short and fun for your dog, they will be eager to learn more.

Photo Credit: Kathi Liebe of Starcreek Frenchies

Adult Activities

When your French Bulldog is a full grown adult (approximately two years of age), now is the time that you can begin more complicated or advanced training sessions. They will enjoy it and when you have the desire and patience, there is no end to the tricks you can teach a willing Frenchie.

Rally Obedience

Rally Obedience (RallyO) is a fun canine sport that is less strict than regular Obedience, in which the dog and guardian (handler) complete a course that has been designed by the rally judge.

The judge signals the handler (or guardian) to begin, and then both dog and guardian begin navigation of the course, at their own pace, which could include anywhere from 10 to 20 stations that require them to perform different tasks.

For instance, a beginner's course may include heel, sits, turns, pace changes, sit-stay, or elements of recall (come). As the dog gains skill, more difficult elements are added into the courses that help to improve you and your dog's performance levels and confidence.

The purpose of RallyO is to promote positive relationships between dogs and owners based on trust and respect.

Everyone can participate, whether purebred show dogs, mixed breeds, handicapped guardians, or 3-legged dogs, because the whole idea is for everyone to have fun together, and every dog and guardian has something special to offer. Currently, the CKC is the only organization that restricts competition to purebred dogs.

Agility

Agility is a fun and fast dog sport in which the dog's guardian or handler directs their off-leash dog through an obstacle course, without food or toys as incentives and without touching either the dog or the obstacles in the course.

Control of the dog is limited to voice, movement, and various body signals, which means that in order for your French Bulldog to be able to successfully compete, they must already know basic commands, such as sit, come, stay, up, and down while they are closely focused on you.

Musical Canine Freestyle

This freestyle, modern dog sport put to music is known by several names, including "musical canine freestyle," "freestyle dance," and "canine freestyle."

This sport, which mixes music with dance and obedience training to allow for fun, entertaining and creative communication between dogs and their handlers or guardians, has become so popular that dogs and humans can now compete in many countries worldwide.

Socialization

Generally speaking, the majority of an adult dog's habits and behavioral traits will be formed between the ages of birth and one year of age.

This is why it will be very important to introduce your French Bulldog puppy to a wide variety of animals, locations, sights, sounds, and smells during this formative period in their young life.

Your French Bulldog puppy will learn how to behave in all these various circumstances by following your lead, feeling your energy, and watching how you react in every situation.

For instance, never accidentally reward your French Bulldog puppy for displaying fear or growling at another dog or animal by picking them up.

Picking up a French Bulldog puppy or dog at this time, when they are displaying unbalanced energy, actually turns out to be a reward for them, and you will be teaching them to continue with this type of behavior.

As well, picking up a puppy literally places them in a "top dog" position, where they are higher and more dominant than the dog or animal they just growled at.

The correct action to take in such a situation is to gently correct your French Bulldog puppy with a firm, yet calm energy by distracting them with a "No," so that they learn to let you deal with the situation on their behalf.

If you allow a fearful or nervous puppy to deal with situations that unnerve them all by themselves, they may learn to react with fear or aggression, and you will have created a problem that could escalate into something quite serious as they grow older. The same is true of situations where a young puppy may feel the need to protect themselves from a bigger or older dog that may come charging in for a sniff.

It is the guardian's responsibility to protect the puppy so that they do not think they must react with fear or aggression in order to protect themselves.

Once your French Bulldog puppy has received all their vaccinations, you can take them out to public dog parks and various locations where many dogs are found.

Before allowing them to interact with other dogs or puppies, take them for a disciplined walk on leash so that they will be a little tired and less likely to immediately engage with all other dogs.

Keep your puppy on leash and close beside you, because most puppies are usually a bundle of out-of-control energy, and you need to protect them while teaching them how far they can go before getting themselves into trouble with adult dogs who may not appreciate excited puppy playfulness.

If your puppy shows any signs of aggression or domination toward another puppy or dog, you must immediately step in and calmly discipline them; by doing nothing, you will be allowing them to get into situations that could become serious behavioral issues.

Take your puppy everywhere with you and introduce them to many different people of all ages, sizes, and ethnicities.

Most people will come to you and want to interact with your puppy. If they ask if they can hold your puppy, let them, because so long as they are gentle and don't drop the puppy, this is a good way to socialize your French Bulldog and show them that humans are friendly.

Do not let others (especially children) play roughly with your puppy or squeal at them in high-pitched voices, because this can be very frightening for a young puppy. As well, you do not want to teach your puppy that humans are a source of excitement.

Be especially careful when introducing your puppy to young children who don't know how to act around a puppy and who may accidentally hurt your puppy. You don't want them to become fearful of children, as this could lead to aggression later on in life.

Explain to children that your French Bulldog puppy is very young and that they must be calm and gentle when playing or interacting in any way.

As important as socialization is, it is also important that the dog be left alone for short periods when young so that they can cope with some periods of isolation. If an owner goes out and they have never experienced this, they can destroy or mess because they panic. They are thinking that they are vulnerable and can be attacked by something or someone coming in to the house.

Dogs that have been socialized are able to easily diffuse a potentially troublesome situation and hence they will rarely get into fights. Dogs that are not poorly socialized often misinterpret or do not understand the subtle signals of other dogs, getting into trouble as a result.

Tricks

When your French Bulldog is accustomed to following basic commands, you are much more likely to get him to respond to cues for "tricks" like shaking hands, rolling over, or similar behaviors. I always suggest catering to some natural tendency the dog has to teach the first trick.

Always offer praise and show pleasure when the dog responds correctly. If you make training just another form of "play," your Frenchie will be an enthusiastic participant.

Playtime

Playtime is important, especially for a dog's natural desire to chase. Try channeling this instinct with toys and games. If a dog has no stimulation and has nothing to chase, they can start to chase their own tail which can lead to problems.

Toys can be used to simulate the dog's natural desire to hunt. For example, when they catch a toy they will often shake it and bury their teeth into it, simulating the killing of their prey.

Allow your dog to fulfill a natural desire to chew. This comes from historically catching their prey and then chewing the carcass. Providing chews or bones can prevent your dog destroying your home.

Our sedentary lifestyle is counter to the dog's natural instinct to hunt and be extremely active. Expecting our pet dogs to lie quietly with the occasional short walk in a day can sometimes leave them with too much energy leading to behavioral problems.

Playing with your dog is not only a great way of getting them to use up their energy but it is also a great way of bonding with them as they have fun. Dogs love to chase and catch balls, just make sure that the ball is too large to be swallowed.

When picking out toys for your French Bulldog regardless of his age, don't get anything soft and "shred-able." Frenchies can be regular engines of destruction!

I recommend small chew toys like Nylabones that can withstand the abuse. You can buy items made out of this tough material in the $1 - $5 / £0.59 - £2.97 range.

Deer antlers are wonderful toys for Frenchies. Most love them. They do not smell, are all-natural, and do not stain or splinter. I recommend the antlers that are not split, as the split ones do not last as long.

Never give your dog rawhide, cow hooves, or pig's ears. The rawhide and pig's ears become soft and present choking hazards, while the cow hooves can splinter and puncture the cheek or palate.

Avoid soft rubber toys that can be chewed into pieces and swallowed, opt for rope toys instead. Don't buy anything with a squeaker or any other part that presents a choking hazard.

Grooming

Do not allow yourself to get caught in the "my dog doesn't like it" trap, which is an excuse many owners will use to avoid regular grooming sessions. When you allow your dog to dictate whether they will permit a grooming session, you are setting a dangerous precedent.

Once you have bonded with your dog they love to be tickled, rubbed, and scratched in certain favorite places. This is why grooming is a great source of pleasure and a way to bond with your pet.

For the most part grooming your French Bulldog means brushing it once a week with a slicker brush, costing less than $10 / £5.94. Since this will be time spent with you, likely in your lap, your Frenchie will be completely onboard with the process!

This is also an excellent opportunity to examine your dog's skin for any growths, lumps, bumps, or wounds and to have a good look at his ears, eyes, and mouth.

Be alert to any changes in color and texture, and look for signs of discharge or, in the case of the ears, accumulated debris in the ear canal and any evidence of a foul or yeasty odor that could indicate the presence of ear mites (which are easily treated with ointment available from your vet).

Typically a French Bulldog won't need a wet bath more than 2-3 times a year unless they get into something and are really dirty. When you do bathe your dog, use a good-quality pet shampoo that is fragrance free and made of natural ingredients only. This will lessen the chance of an allergic reaction.

Do not get your pet's head and ears wet, or use shampoo in those areas. Instead, clean your Frenchie's head and face with a warm, wet wash cloth only, and use a cotton swab to clean between the creases of skin on his forehead and face.

You may have to clean the facial creases on a more regular basis, depending on the dog's level of activity and your climate. Just watch that area closely for an accumulation of dirt to set up a separate schedule to tend to this chore.

Be sure to thoroughly rinse your dog's coat with clean, fresh water to remove all residues. Towel your pet dry and make sure he doesn't get chilled.

Fleas and Ticks

If you are going to have a dog for a pet, the time will come when you find a flea — or as I like to call them, a "passenger" — on your pet. This is not the dog's fault, nor is it the end of the world.

Certainly you want to deal with the problem immediately, but in the short term, the flea is far happier on the dog than it would be on you.

NEVER treat a puppy of less than 12 weeks of age with a commercial flea product and be extremely careful of using these items on adult dogs as well. Most of the major brand products contain pyrethrum, which has been responsible for adverse reactions in small dogs to the point of being fatal. Others have recovered, but suffered life-long neurological damage.

The very best thing you can do to get rid of fleas is to give your dog a bath in warm water using a standard canine shampoo. Comb the animal's fur with a fine-toothed flea comb. Any live fleas that you collect in the comb will die when you submerge the comb in hot soapy water.

Photo Credit: Kathi Liebe of Starcreek Frenchies

Wash all of the dog's bedding and any soft materials with which he has come in contact in hot water. Look for any accumulations of "flea dirt," which is actually excreted blood from adult fleas.

Expect to continue washing the bedding and other surfaces daily for at least a week. You are trying to remove any remaining eggs so that no new fleas hatch out.

If you find a tick on your dog, you can remove the blood-sucking parasite by first coating it with a thick layer of petroleum jelly. Leave this on for up to 5 minutes. The jelly clogs the spiracles through which the tick breathes and causes its jaws to release. You can then simply pluck the tick off with a pair of tweezers with a straight motion.

Never just jerk a tick off a dog. The head of the creature will be left behind and will continue to burrow into the skin making a painful sore.

Nail Trimming

Even if you routinely walk your dog on asphalt or other rough surfaces, their nails will likely not stay ground-down adequately enough to avoid regular nail trimming as a routine grooming chore.

Always use a nail trimmer designed for use with dogs. I prefer the kind with plier grips, as they are easier to handle and are inexpensive, selling for under $20 / £11.88

French Bulldogs can be stubborn, and may not like to have their paws handled, so it's good to start this routine as early in life as possible. So long as the dog doesn't struggle, clipping the nails is as simple as snipping off the nail tips at a 45-degree angle.

Be careful not to cut too far down for fear of catching the vascular quick, which will hurt the dog and bleed profusely. If you have never done this chore before and are nervous or apprehensive, ask your vet or a professional groomer to walk you through it the first time.

I really recommend using one of the "Dremel" type hand held grinders for nails. It is basically just a rotating emery wheel. No issues with pinching their nails as with a "chopper" type nail clipper. Only use a slow speed Dremel, such as Model 7300-PT Pet Nail Grooming Tool (approx. $40/£20).

Anal Glands

If your French Bulldog has an episode of diarrhea, or if the animal's stools tend to be soft, the sacs on either side of the anus, the anal glands, may become blocked and foul smelling.

Signs that a dog has blocked anal glands typically include scooting or rubbing the bottom on the ground or carpet.

If this occurs, the glands will need to be expressed to prevent an abscess from forming. This is a sensitive task and one that a veterinarian should perform.

Interested in Showing Your Pet?

If you have purchased a show-quality French Bulldog and are planning to enter the world of dog shows and the dog fancy, you have a whole education in front of you that is outside the purview of this book.

If you have not already done so, you will want to begin to attend dog shows and to make connections in the world of the dog fancy to acquire the training to participate with your dog, or to hire someone to show the animal for you.

What Dogs are Qualified to Participate?

For a dog to participate in a dog show, it must be registered with the governing body for that exhibition. For instance, dogs registered with the American Kennel Club that are 6 months or older on the day of the show are eligible to enter AKC sponsored events. Spayed or neutered dogs are not eligible, nor are dogs with disqualifying faults according to the accepted standard for the breed.

Joining a Breed Club

When you attend a dog show, find out about joining a breed-specific club in your area. Such groups usually sponsor classes to teach the basics in handling and showing the breed or will have contacts to put you in touch with individual teachers.

Breed club membership is also important to learn the culture of the dog fancy and to meet people in the show world. You will begin by participating in smaller, local shows to learn the ropes before entering an event that will garner points toward sanctioned titles within a governing group's system.

Hiring a Professional

It is not uncommon for people who own show quality animals to hire professional handlers to work with the dogs, for a fee.

If you are interested in going this route, be sure to interview several handlers and to get a full schedule of their rates. Attend a show where they are working with a dog and watch them in action. Ask for references, and contact the people whose names you are given.

Entrusting a handler with the care of your dog is an enormous leap of faith. You want to be certain you have hired someone with whom you are completely comfortable and with whom your dog has an observable rapport.

Breeding French Bulldogs

It is not recommended that French Bulldog owners attempt to breed their pets. Only professional breeders with advanced knowledge of the breed should undertake this process, since both artificial insemination and delivery via Caesarian are the standards of Frenchie reproduction.

Dogs that are selected to participate in breeding programs:

- Have a pedigree that is traceable through 3-5 generations.
- Exhibit exceptional temperament and socialize well with people and other animals.
- Have no known genetic defects in regard to their respiratory and skeletal systems, in particular the spinal column.
- Do not have any orthopedic issues including hip dysplasia and luxation of the patella.
- Conform as closely as possible to the recognized breed standard.
- Have tested free of any infectious disease.
- Is a female dog two years of age or older in at least her second heat cycle.

Only those individuals with knowledge of the breed and the financial wherewithal to provide veterinary care should ever become breeders, and then only for the purpose of improving the breed.

The French Bull Dog Club of America's Code of Ethics states, "I will breed a bitch only with the intent that this particular breeding will improve the breed."

That means the only goal of the mating is to produce puppies that are in sound health and improve the conformation of the line — not as a scheme to make money.

Regardless of the cost of purebred French Bulldog puppies, most honest breeders will tell you that when all of their expenses are met, they barely break even.

Photo Credit: Kathi Liebe of Starcreek Frenchies

Chapter 5 – French Bulldog Health

It's impossible to emphasize strongly enough that in all phases of your dog's life, you are your pet's best healthcare. I always tell owners that no one will know their French Bulldog the way they do. If you think something is wrong, it probably is.

To that end, learning the fundamentals of preventive health care and understanding the health issues commonly associated with this breed will help you to monitor your Frenchie's wellbeing and to make good decisions on his behalf.

Working with Your Veterinarian

If you do not already have a veterinarian with whom you work, finding a qualified doctor is the first step in ensuring your dog's long-term good health. Ask your breeder for a recommendation, or if you have worked with a kennel outside of your immediate area, try to connect with other French Bulldog owners in your locale.

If this is not possible, and the vet you are considering has not treated a French Bulldog before, ask if any of their patients have been pugs, English or American bulldogs, or Boston terriers. They are all brachycephalic breeds (dogs with dramatically short and flat noses) and are prone to developing similar health issues as French Bulldogs.

Make an appointment to go into the clinic to see the facility and meet the vet. Be clear that you are there to discuss becoming a client and will happily pay the fee for a visit. Prepare your questions in advance so you don't waste anyone's time — including your own. Some questions you will want answered include:

- How long has your clinic been open?
- What hours do you operate?
- What medical services do you offer?
- What grooming services do you offer?
- Do you have an estimated schedule of fees?
- How many vets are on staff?
- Do you provide emergency services after hours?
- Is there an emergency vet clinic you recommend?
- Are there any specialists in your practice?
- Where do you refer dogs in need of a specialist?
- Do you currently treat any French Bulldogs?
- Do you treat any brachycephalic breeds?

Pay attention to how you are greeted when you arrive at the clinic. Does the staff seem friendly and approachable? Are they well organized? Is there a bulletin board in the waiting room with notes and photos from patients? If so, that's always a good sign of a satisfied clientele. Does the facility seem modern and up-to-date? Is it clean, airy, and light? Are the doctor's credentials prominently displayed?

First Visit to the Vet

If you are satisfied with the answers you receive and what you see on your tour of the clinic, schedule a second visit to come in with your puppy. Bring all medical records with you since you will likely be discussing completing the dog's required vaccinations and arranging to have him spayed or neutered.

The routine examination will include a reading on the dog's temperature and a check of heart and lung function with a stethoscope. The puppy will be weighed and measured for its permanent record. If you have any questions about French Bulldog health moving forward, try to have them prepared in advance so you don't forget anything.

Vaccinations

A usual course of vaccinations begins when a puppy is 6-7 weeks of age. The first shot is a combination inoculation for distemper, hepatitis, parvovirus, parainfluenza, and coronavirus.

Boosters are administered at 9, 12, and 16 weeks. Depending on the area, a vaccine for Lyme Disease may be started at 16 weeks, with a booster required at 18 weeks.

The rabies vaccination is administered at 12-16 weeks of age and annually for life thereafter.

DAPP Vaccinations

All puppies are vaccinated by a licensed veterinarian in order to provide them with protection against the four most common and serious diseases, which include Distemper, Adenovirus, Parainfluenza, and Parvovirus. This set of four primary vaccinations is referred to as "DAPP."

Approximately one week after your French Bulldog puppy has completed all three sets of DAPP vaccinations, they will be fully protected from these four specific diseases. Then, most veterinarians will recommend a once-a-year vaccination for the next year or two.

Distemper

Canine distemper is a contagious and serious viral illness for which there is currently no known cure.

This deadly virus, which is spread either through the air or by direct or indirect contact with a dog that is already infected, or other distemper carrying wildlife, including ferrets, raccoons, foxes, skunks, and wolves, is a relative of the measles virus that affects humans.

Canine distemper is sometimes also called "hard pad disease" because some strains of the distemper virus actually cause thickening of the pads on a dog's feet, which can also affect the end of a dog's nose.

In dogs or animals with weak immune systems, death may result two to five weeks after the initial infection.

Early symptoms of distemper include fever, loss of appetite, and mild eye inflammation that may only last a day or two. Symptoms become more serious and noticeable as the disease progresses.

Photo Credit: Kathi Liebe of Starcreek Frenchies

A puppy or dog that survives the distemper virus will usually continue to experience symptoms or signs of the disease throughout their remaining lifespan, including "hard pad disease" as well as "enamel hypoplasia," which is damage to the enamel of the puppy's teeth that are not yet formed or that have not yet pushed through the gums.

Enamel hypoplasia is caused by the distemper virus killing the cells that manufacture tooth enamel.

Adenovirus

This virus causes infectious canine hepatitis, which can range in severity from very mild to very serious, or even cause death.

Symptoms can include coughing, loss of appetite, increased thirst and urination, tiredness, runny eyes and nose, vomiting, bruising or bleeding under the skin, swelling of the head, neck and trunk, fluid accumulation in the abdomen area, jaundice (yellow tinge to the skin), a bluish clouding of the cornea of the eye (called "hepatitis blue eye"), and seizures.

There is no specific treatment for infectious canine hepatitis, and treatment is focused on managing symptoms while the virus runs its course. Hospitalization and intravenous fluid therapy may be required in severe cases.

Parainfluenza Virus

The canine parainfluenza virus originally affected only horses but has now adapted to become contagious to dogs. Also referred to as "canine influenza virus," "greyhound disease," or "race flu," it is easily spread from dog to dog through the air or by coming into contact with respiratory secretions from an infected animal.

While the more frequent occurrences of this respiratory infection are seen in areas with high dog populations, such as race tracks, boarding kennels, and pet stores, this virus is highly contagious to any dog or puppy, regardless of age.

Symptoms can include a dry, hacking cough, difficulty breathing, wheezing, runny nose and eyes, sneezing, fever, loss of appetite, tiredness, depression, and possible pneumonia.

In cases where only a cough exists, tests will be required to determine whether the cause of the cough is the parainfluenza virus or the less serious "kennel cough."

While many dogs can naturally recover from this virus, they will remain contagious. For this reason, to prevent the spread to other animals, aggressive treatment of the virus with antibiotics and antiviral drugs will be the prescribed course of action.

In more severe cases, a cough suppressant may be used, as well as intravenous fluids to prevent secondary bacterial infection.

Parvovirus

Canine parvovirus is a highly contagious viral illness affecting puppies and dogs that also affects other canine species, including foxes, coyotes, and wolves.

There are two forms of this virus — (1) the more common intestinal form and (2) the less common cardiac form, which can cause death in young puppies.

Symptoms of the intestinal form of parvovirus include vomiting, bloody diarrhea, weight loss, and lack of appetite, while the less common cardiac form attacks the heart muscle.

Early vaccination in young puppies has radically reduced the incidence of canine parvovirus infection, which is easily transmitted either by direct contact with an infected dog, or indirectly, by sniffing an infected dog's feces.

The virus can also be brought into a dog's environment on the bottom of human shoes that may have stepped on infected feces, and there is evidence that this hardy virus can live in ground soil for up to a year.

Recovery from parvovirus requires both aggressive and early treatment. With proper treatment, death rates are relatively low (between 5 and 20%), although chances of survival for puppies are much lower than older dogs, and in all instances, there is no guarantee of survival.

Treatment of parvovirus requires hospitalization where intravenous fluids and nutrients are administered to help combat dehydration. As well, antibiotics will be given to counteract secondary bacterial infections, and as necessary, medications to control nausea and vomiting may be given.

Without prompt and proper treatment, dogs that have severe parvovirus infections can die within 48 to 72 hours.

Rabies Vaccinations

Rabies is a viral disease transmitted through the saliva of an infected animal, usually through a bite. The virus travels to the brain along the nerves, and once symptoms develop, death is almost certainly inevitable, usually following a prolonged period of suffering.

I highly recommend that the rabies vaccine be given separately, by at least a few days, from all other vaccines. I know of several Frenchies who had reactions to the combined vaccines.

Leishmaniasis

Leishmaniasis is caused by a parasite and is transmitted by a bite from a sand fly. There is no definitive answer for effectively combating leishmaniasis, especially since one vaccine will not prevent the known multiple species.

Note: Leishmaniasis is a "zoonotic" infection, which means that this is a contagious disease, and that organisms residing in the Leishmaniasis lesions can be spread between animals and humans and, ultimately, transmitted to humans.

Lyme Disease

This is one of the most common tick-borne diseases in the world, which is transmitted by Borrelia bacteria found in the deer or sheep tick. Lyme disease, also called "borreliosis," can affect both humans and dogs, and can be fatal.

There is a vaccine for Lyme disease, and dogs living in areas that have easy access to these ticks should be vaccinated yearly.

Photo Credit: Suirac French Bulldogs & Epic French Bulldogs

Evaluating for Worms

Before your puppy's first visit with the vet, you will be asked to collect a fresh stool sample, which will be tested for worms. If any parasites are found, the puppy will be given an initial deworming agent, followed by a second course in 10 days, to make sure any remaining eggs have been killed.

It is unlikely that a puppy purchased from a breeder will have worms, but a rescue dog might. Typically, the only external signs of roundworms are small white granules around the anus. Other worms can only be detected with microscopic examination. Tapeworms in particular can be life threatening and require veterinary treatment.

De-worming kills internal parasites that your dog or puppy has, and no matter where you live, how sanitary your conditions, or how much of a neat freak you are, your dog will have internal parasites, because it is not a matter of cleanliness.

It is recommended by the Centers for Disease Control and Prevention (CDC) that puppies be de-wormed every 2 weeks until they are 3 months old, and then every month after that in order to control worms.

Many veterinarians recommend worming dogs for tapeworm and roundworms every 6-12 months.

Spaying and Neutering

Spaying or neutering your French Bulldog puppy is typically a requirement of the adoption agreement. These procedures, however, beyond eliminating unwanted pregnancies, also carry significant health benefits for your pet.

Neutered males face a reduced risk of prostatic disease or perianal tumors. The surgery also reduces many aggressive behaviors and lessens the dog's territorial instinct. He will be less likely to mark territory, or to behave inappropriately against the legs of your visitors.

Spayed females no longer face the prospect of uterine or ovarian cancer and have a diminished risk for breast cancer. You will not have to deal with your pet coming into season, nor will she experience hormonally-related mood swings.

Neutering and spaying surgeries are typically performed around six months of age. The procedures don't make the dogs any more prone to gain weight. Frenchies are already notorious for packing on the pounds. Regulating their diet is an absolute must of basic healthcare for the breed.

"Normal" Health Issues

Although French Bulldogs are, on a whole, happy and healthy, there are some issues that can arise that should be treated by or evaluated by a veterinarian to be on the safe side. Anytime that your dog seems inattentive or lethargic and stops eating or drinking water, seek medical attention for your pet immediately.

Note: Any gastrointestinal upset in dogs can be linked to ingestion of toxic household or garden plants.

Diarrhea

French Bulldog puppies have sensitive digestive systems that can be upset by any disruption in their diet, from eating human food to getting into the garbage. This will result in diarrhea (watery and frequent bowel movements).

Typically an instance of diarrhea caused by one of these factors will resolve on its own within 24 hours after the offending food has passed out of the animal's system.

During episodes of diarrhea, give your puppy only small amounts of dry food and do not include any treats. It is imperative the puppy have access to fresh, clean water. If the condition has not improved in 24 hours, take the dog to the vet.

Even adult dogs will sometimes have occasional gastrointestinal upset that manifests as diarrhea. Typically this is not a serious health concern so long as the episode resolves in a day. Any chronic or prolonged condition, however, is another matter.

For chronic, episodic diarrhea, the cause is typically dietary and often linked to an over-abundance of rich, fatty food. Try switching to a food that is lower in fat, with less protein. Smaller portions and more frequent feedings are also indicated.

If you suspect that the cause of the upset is an allergy, consider having your dog tested so you can find the right food. Many small dogs are allergic to chicken and turkey, for instance.

There is always the possibility that the diarrhea is being caused by some pathogen, either a bacteria or a virus. If vomiting and a fever are also present, your pet is likely suffering from an infection and requires veterinary attention.

Finally, your dog may need to be wormed. Both tapeworm and roundworm can cause instances of diarrhea.

Vomiting

Vomiting, like diarrhea, may also be a sign of a change in diet or an indication that the puppy has gotten into something that didn't agree with him. So long as the dog is actually throwing up and getting the substance out of his system, the issue should resolve in about 24 hours.

However, if the dog is attempting to vomit and cannot expel anything, if there's any trace of blood in the material that is expelled, or if your pet cannot even keep water down, call the vet immediately. Dehydration is a dangerous and potentially fatal condition and may require the administration of intravenous fluids.

Always examine the area where the dog has been and try to identify anything with signs of chewing, or any item that is missing and might have been swallowed. This may help both you and the vet to get a handle on the cause of the dog's illness.

Other potential causes of vomiting include the presence of hookworm or roundworm, pancreatitis (inflammation of the pancreas), diabetes, thyroid disease, kidney disease, liver disease, or some sort of physical obstruction that has caused a blockage. In this latter instance, surgery may be necessary.

In cases of both diarrhea and/or vomiting, you can add white rice to your dog's regular food after 48 hours to improve the consistency of the stools and to settle ongoing stomach upset. Generally you can resume your pet's regular diet after 72 hours.

Bloat

Bloat occurs when a puppy eats too quickly and, in the process, swallows large amounts of air that fills up the stomach and causes it to become swollen. If the stomach turns gastric torsion, the flow of blood in the abdomen will be cut off, causing shock and death.

The symptoms of bloat include distension of the abdomen; dry vomiting, and coughing after eating. If you suspect your puppy is suffering from bloat, seek the aid of a qualified veterinary professional immediately.

Bloat can be avoided by feeding the dog several small meals each day in a quiet, distraction-free environment and by not allowing the animal to exercise for at least an hour after eating.

Allergies

Dogs of any age can suffer from allergies. These may be either environmental or substance-based to items like cleaning solutions, laundry soap, or fabric softeners. Puppies come into contact with this type of chemical most often in their bedding, but they can also rub against things in your home and be exposed to the irritant.

Typical canine responses to allergic reactions include scratching, licking, and chewing, but this behavior will differ from a response to fleas. With "passengers" the dog will scratch or chew intermittently, but with allergies, they will worry at the spot constantly, often causing patches of hair loss and the eruption of skin rashes.

If possible, identify and remove the irritants causing the problem. Begin by washing your dog's bedding in perfume-free detergent and do not use dryer sheets. If anything new has come into the house against which the dog might be rubbing, temporarily remove the item. Also, if you have switched to a new brand or flavor of food, go back to what the puppy was eating previously.

In instances where you cannot discover the source of the irritation, it may be necessary to take the dog in for allergy testing. It is possible your pet will need antihistamines to provide relief and stop the chewing and scratching.

Signs of Illness

Any of the following symptoms may indicate the presence of a more serious medical problem. If your dog exhibits any of these behaviors, you should have the animal evaluated immediately. Delay may allow a condition that could be treated and resolved to become chronic.

Coughing and/or Wheezing

All dogs cough occasionally, but if your French Bulldog exhibits this symptom for more than a week, take him in to see the vet. Coughing in French Bulldogs is not a disease, but a symptom of a more serious medical problem. An occasional cough is completely normal, but when it lasts more than a few weeks, it is time for a trip to your veterinarian.

The breed's flat face makes them especially prone to respiratory issues. A cough can indicate a number of conditions, including kennel cough, heartworm, cardiac disease, bacterial infections, parasites, tumors, and allergies.

Kennel cough presents with a hacking, dry cough. It is often the result of a dog having been boarded in overly warm, crowded conditions with poor airflow. Typically kennel cough will resolve on its own, but it is still important that the dog be seen by a vet for recommendations to ease symptoms. A cough suppressant may be required, and often a humidifier in the room will soothe the irritated airways.

In cases where the origin of the cough is uncertain, the vet will take a full medical history, order blood work and x-rays, and test your pet for heartworms. If necessary, a fluid sample taken from the lungs will help to identify any infections present.

In addition to coughing, be alert for signs of labored breathing and wheezing. This can be a sign of accumulated fluid in the chest or lungs. French Bulldogs are known for making a wide range of "snarfling" noises, including coughing and snorting.

It can be difficult to tell what is "normal" and what is of medical concern. Take into consideration your pet's overall demeanor and appetite, but don't fail to go in to the vet for fear of being seen as an over-reacting "parent." It's always best to err on the side of caution.

A Note on Heartworms

Heartworms are thin, long worms that live in the cardiac muscle and cause bleeding and blocked blood vessels. The presence of these parasites can lead to heart failure and death. Coughing and fainting, as well as an intolerance to exercise, are all symptoms of heartworm. The parasite, *Dirofilaria Immitis*, is transmitted by a mosquito bite. You should discuss heartworm prevention with your vet and, together, decide on the best course of action to keep your pet safe.

Bad Breath and Dental Care

While bad breath or halitosis is not a health problem per se, it can be an indication of dental issues, like an over-accumulation of plaque or periodontal disease like gingivitis. Regular dental exams by the vet and brushing your pet's teeth daily will help to prevent these problems.

Your vet's office should carry "finger brushes," canine-specific toothpaste, and dental chews. Using these products does not replace regular dental cleanings, but they are very helpful. Ask your vet to demonstrate the proper way to brush your dog's teeth, and start early. Puppies are much more agreeable to the process than older dogs.

Other problems that may lead to bad breath include sinus infections, canine diabetes, tonsillitis, respiratory disease, kidney disease, liver disease, gastrointestinal blockages, and even cancer. Always consult with your vet in instances of chronic and unresolved halitosis.

Other Warning Signs

In addition to these warning signs of potential illness, also be on the lookout for:

- Excessive and unexplained drooling.
- Excessive consumption of water and increased urination.
- Changes in appetite leading to weight gain or loss.
- Marked change in levels of activity.
- Disinterest in favorite activities.
- Stiffness and difficulty standing or climbing stairs.
- Sleeping more than normal.
- Shaking of the head.
- Any sores, lumps, or growths.
- Dry, red, or cloudy eyes.

Often the signs of serious illness are subtle. Again, trust your instincts. You know your dog. If you think something is wrong, do not hesitate to consult with your vet.

Genetic Abnormalities and Conditions

There are a number of genetic abnormalities and conditions common to French Bulldogs. Most are associated with their heavy build, short legs, and flat faces.

Brachycephalic Airway Syndrome

French Bulldogs are brachycephalic, meaning their skull bones are shortened, giving their face and nose a pushed in or flat appearance. This changes the anatomy and relationship of many soft tissue structures associated with breathing and can lead to brachycephalic airway syndrome.

The most common abnormalities seen are stenotic nares, an elongated soft palate, a hypoplastic trachea, and everted laryngeal saccules. In layman's terms, this translates to abnormally small or narrow nostrils, a soft palate that is too long for the length of the mouth and may block the entrance to the trachea, which itself can be too small in diameter.

Laryngeal saccules are small sacs or pouches in the larynx that if everted, turn outward and have a tendency to get sucked into the airway, further obstructing the flow of respiration.

Dogs with brachycephalic airway syndrome can breathe most easily through their mouths, but they may make a lot of respiratory noise, including snorting when excited and snoring when relaxed. They may tire easily when exercised or even faint and collapse from too much exertion. Coughing, retching, gagging, and vomiting are common and are made worse by hot, humid weather.

Over time, secondary problems will develop, including inflammation to the airways and strain to the heart from the exertion associated with breathing.

Spinal Issues

Back and spinal disease are definitely an issue with French Bulldogs. Congenital deformities of the vertebrae can place pressure on the spinal cord that causes chronic pain, malfunction of the hind legs, and incontinence.

Responsible breeders x-ray puppies at around 10-12 weeks of age to eliminate any bad backs from their breeding program.

Hemivertebrae are very common with Frenchies. Essentially, one half of the vertebral body does not develop properly, resulting in a wedge shape. Typically 2-4 vertebrae on a single dog will be affected. If there is no kinking of the spine or trouble with the hindquarters, the dog can lead a full and active life, but is not a candidate for a breeding program.

Patella Luxation

A patella luxation is a dislocation of a dog's "kneecap," which is the small bone that protects the front of the stifle joint in the hind leg. This joint is located between the thigh and upper leg, halfway between the hock and the pelvis.

Ligaments hold the patella in place and keep it in position during movement when it slides along a groove in the femur bone. It may move out of place toward the inside (medial) or outside (lateral) portions of the leg as a consequence of injury or as a congenital deformity.

Medial patella luxation is common in bulldogs as a birth defect, and is, in fact, one of the five most common birth defects in all dog breeds. Severity is graded on a scale of 1 to 4. In Grade 1, the patella pops out without pain and can be massaged back in place. Grade 2 cases experience pain and, although the patella can be re-positioned, it dislocates again with movement. Grades 3 and 4 cause mobility problems and discomfort severe enough to warrant surgery.

Hip Dysplasia

Hip dysplasia typically presents in middle-aged or elderly dogs, but can surface as soon as six months of age. The condition varies from mild to debilitating but luckily is not common to Frenchies. Bulldog hips are less deep and jointed differently. It gives a different gait. Most Frenchies are athletic and leap upon furniture at times.

Hypothyroidism

Hypothyroidism is an endocrine disorder prevalent in French Bulldogs. In its congenital (juvenile) form, hypothyroidism can present as early as five months of age. If present, it can kill pups before they are ever weaned. For this reason, breeders routinely check their litters for hypothyroidism before puppies are made available for purchase.

Primary hypothyroidism in adult Frenchies is more common, and is caused either by an autoimmune reaction or is idiopathic.

Symptoms include hair loss and a thinning of the coat as well as obesity. The condition is treated with hormones and requires regular monitoring. Typically after 6 weeks of treatment, hypothyroidism can be brought under control successfully.

Entropion

Entropion, or "diamond eye," occurs when the dog's eyelids and the hair surrounding the eye turns inward, scratching the cornea. If left untreated, permanent scarring and loss of vision may occur.

Distichiasis is a similar condition with the same results, but is caused by the presence of a double row of eyelashes.

Because both conditions are uncomfortable, affected dogs will rub their eyes, causing greater damage and chronic eye infections. Surgical intervention is highly successful in resolving the issue and should be performed as soon as possible to protect your pet's sight.

Note: French Bulldogs, like all bulldogs, are sometimes prone to a bulging of the tear gland called "cherry eye." This is also a condition requiring veterinary treatment and potentially surgery.

Health Emergency: Heat Stroke

Heat stroke is a serious health emergency in French Bulldogs and should be avoided at all costs. Dogs do not have sweat glands and manage their bodily cooling through their tongue, nose, and paw pads. Frenchies have a greatly diminished capacity to regulate their body temperature and will collapse in high humidity and excessive heat. If your pet does not receive immediate assistance, heat stroke can be fatal.

Signs of heat stroke include:

- fatigue
- excessive panting
- heavy salivation
- muscle tremors
- rapid breathing
- staggering

As the condition progresses the animal may experience convulsions, vomiting, and diarrhea before collapsing.

At the first sign of heatstroke, get your French Bulldog into a cool or shady area. Soak your pet in cool, not cold water. Do NOT cover the dog with a wet towel. This will actually prevent the escape of heat from the animal's body. Fan your dog to encourage evaporation of the water to aid in cooling. Call the vet and get your pet in for treatment as quickly as possible.

Photo Credit: Kathi Liebe of Starcreek Frenchies

Chapter 6 - Growing Older

As a result of advances in veterinary care, improvements in diet and nutrition, and general knowledge concerning proper care of our canine companions, our dogs are able to enjoy longer, healthier lives, and as such, when caring for them we need to be aware of behavioral and physical changes that will affect our dogs as they approach old age.

Dogs do not age any more predictably than humans do. You can expect to see conditions like arthritis and cataracts, as well as a gradual diminishment of abilities like vision and hearing.

Older pets also are prone to benign fatty tumors called lipomas. All lumps, bumps, and growths should, however, still be evaluated by your vet.

Physiological Changes

As our beloved canine companions become senior dogs, they will be suffering from physical aging problems similar to those that affect humans, such as heightened sensitivity to cold and hot weather, pain, stiffness and arthritis, diminished or complete loss of hearing and sight, and inability to control their bowels and bladder. Any of these problems will reduce a dog's willingness to want to exercise.

Behavioral Changes

Further, a senior French Bulldog may experience behavioral changes resulting from loss of hearing and sight, such as disorientation, fear or startle reactions, and overall grumpiness from any number of physical problems that could be causing them pain whenever they move.

Just as research and science has improved our human quality of life in our senior years, the same is becoming true for our canine counterparts, who are able to benefit from dietary supplements and pharmaceutical products to help them be as comfortable as possible in their advancing years.

Of course there will be some inconveniences associated with keeping a dog with advancing years around the home, however, your French Bulldog deserves no less than to spend their final days in your loving care after they have unconditionally given you their entire lives.

Being aware of the changes that are likely occurring in a senior dog will help you to better care for them during their geriatric years.

Photo Credit: Kathi Liebe of Starcreek Frenchies

For instance, most dogs will experience hearing loss and visual impairment, and depending upon which goes first (hearing or sight) you will need to alter how you communicate. For instance, if a dog's hearing is compromised, then using more hand signals will be helpful.

Deaf dogs will still be able to hear louder noises and feel vibrations, therefore hand clapping, knocking on furniture or walls, using a loud clicker, or stomping your foot on the floor may be a way to get their attention.

If a senior dog loses their eyesight, most dogs will still be able to easily navigate their familiar surroundings, and you will only need to be extra watchful on their behalf when taking them to unfamiliar territory.

If they still have their hearing, you will be able to assist your dog with verbal cues and commands. Dogs that have lost both their hearing and their sight will need to be close to you so that they can relax and not feel nervous, and so that you can communicate by touching parts of their body.

Generally speaking, even when a dog becomes blind and/or deaf, their powerful sense of smell is still functioning, which means that they will be able to smell where you are and navigate their environment by using their nose.

More Frequent Bathroom Breaks

Bathroom breaks may need to become more frequent in older dogs that may lose their ability to hold it for longer periods of time, so be prepared to be more watchful and to offer them opportunities to go outside more frequently during the day.

You may also want to place a pee pad near the door in case they just can't hold it long enough, or if you have not already taught them to bathroom on an indoor potty patch, or pee pad, now may be the time for this alternative bathroom arrangement.

A dog who has been house trained for years will feel the shame and upset of not being able to hold it long enough to get to their regular bathroom location, so be kind and do whatever you need to do to help them not to have to feel bad about failing bowel or bladder control.

Cognitive Decline

Our pets may also begin to show signs of cognitive decline or disorientation and changes in the way their brain functions, similar to what happens to humans suffering from Alzheimer's, where they start to wander about aimlessly, sometimes during the middle of the night.

Make sure that if this is happening with your French Bulldog at nighttime, that they cannot accidentally harm themselves by falling down stairs or getting into areas where they could injure themselves.

Regular Checkups

During this time in your French Bulldog's life, when their immune systems become weakened and they may be experiencing pain, you will want to get into the habit of taking your senior Frenchie for regular vet checkups.

Take them for a checkup every six months so that early detection of any problems can quickly be attended to and solutions for helping to keep them comfortable can be provided.

No Rough Play

An older French Bulldog will not have the same energy or willingness to play that they did when they were younger, therefore, do not allow younger children to rough-house with an older dog.

Explain to children that they must learn to be gentle and to leave the dog alone when it may want to rest or sleep.

Mild Exercise

Dogs still love going for walks, even when they are getting older and may be slowing down.

Even though an older French Bulldog will generally have less energy, they still need to exercise, and taking them out regularly for shorter walks will not only make them happy, keeping them moving will help them to live longer and healthier golden years.

Best Quality Food

Everyone has heard the saying "you are what you eat," and for a senior dog, what they eat is even more important, as their digestive system may no longer be functioning at peak performance.

Feeding a high quality, protein-based food will be important for your senior French Bulldog's continued health.

Note: If your older French Bulldog is overweight, you will want to help them shed excess pounds that will be placing undue stress on their joints and heart. Feed smaller quantities of a higher quality food to help them lose the excess weight.

Clean and Bug Free

The last thing an aging French Bulldog should have to deal with is the misery of itching and scratching, so make sure that you continue to give them regular baths with the appropriate shampoos and conditioners to keep their coat and skin comfortable and free from dirt or invading parasites.

Plenty of Water

Hydration is essential for helping to keep an older French Bulldog comfortable.

Water is life-giving for every creature, so make certain that your aging dog has easy access to plenty of clean, fresh water that will help to improve their energy and digestion and also prevent dehydration, which can add to joint stiffness.

Keeping Warm

Just as older humans feel the cold more, so do older dogs. Keeping your senior French Bulldog warm will help to alleviate some of the pain of their joint stiffness or arthritis.

If there is a draft in the home, generally it will be at floor level, therefore, a bed (ideally heated) that is raised up off of the floor will be warmer for your senior French Bulldog.

While many dogs seem to be happy with sleeping on the floor, providing them with a padded, soft bed will greatly help to relieve sore spots and joint pain in older dogs.

Your aging French Bulldog will be more sensitive to extremes in temperature, therefore, make sure that they are comfortable at all times, which means not too hot and not too cold.

Just like humans, aging dogs have more difficulty maintaining a comfortable body temperature.

Therefore, while you most likely already have a selection of outdoor clothing appropriate to the various climate conditions in which you live, you may not have considered keeping your Frenchie warm while inside the home.

Now would be the time to consider doggy t-shirts or sweater clothing options to help keep your aging companion comfortably warm both inside and out.

Steps or Stairs

If your French Bulldog is allowed to sleep on the human couch or chair, but they are having difficulties getting up there because their joints are becoming stiff and painful, consider buying or making them a set of soft foam stairs so that they can easily get up to their favorite snoozing spot.

More Love and Attention

Last, but not least, make sure that you give your senior French Bulldog lots of love and attention and never leave them alone for long periods of time.

When they are not feeling their best, they will want to be with you all that much more, because you are their guardian whom they trust and love beyond life itself.

Canine Arthritis

As they age, French Bulldogs often develop osteoarthritis. The cartilage in the joints breaks down and the bones rub painfully against each other with no protective buffer. Overweight pets face a significantly higher risk of joint degeneration.

There is no cure for arthritis, but working in partnership with your vet, you can manage your pet's condition with medications and other treatments to reduce inflammation and relieve pain. This may include a weight loss program and even alternative treatments like acupuncture.

Cataracts

All older pets are subject to the development of cataracts, which are microscopic calcium deposits on the lens of the eye. This creates a cloudiness that reduces the ability of light to enter the lens and be processed into a picture on the retina. Cataracts may be a minor annoyance or they can lead to blindness.

Cataracts can occur in one eye only, or in both eyes but at different times. Typically cataracts are not treated in pets, but are simply monitored, with accommodations in the dog's environment as needed to facilitate safe movement around the house.

Euthanasia

End of life decisions for our pets are some of the toughest choices any animal lover can make. No one can or should tell you what to do in this regard.

At those times when I have had to make the choice to aid a pet into a peaceful and pain free transition, I have been extremely fortunate to have the advice and counsel of veterinary professionals who cared about me as well as my animal.

I can't emphasize strongly enough how important it is to have a vet you trust and with whom you can talk. My vet cared for me as much as she cared for my dogs and cats, and knew that I had one criterion in making my health care decisions — is the animal suffering and is there anything you can do to help?

I will confess I have gone to financial extremes in caring for my animals and I have witnessed others do the same. I will not soon forget the day at a veterinary oncology practice when I watched a mountain of a man in black leather hugging a three-legged German Shepherd to his chest and crying with joy because the vet had just said the magic words, "We got it all."

That tough biker sold his Harley to save his dog's life. When someone commented on his sacrifice, he said, still holding his dog, "He's my brother. He'd have done it for me." We all smiled and understood exactly what he meant.

I learned something else in that vet clinic. For the most part, our pets don't know when they have a fatal illness, nor do they mourn the passing of the years as we humans do. The great gift of their existence is a life lived completely in the present — and completely present. We often suffer far more than they do.

You must make the best decision that you can for your pet, but from my perspective, that last decision, to relieve the suffering of a beloved pet at the end of his life, is a great act of love. I think they know that.

When the time comes, euthanasia, or putting a dog "to sleep," will usually be a two-step process.

First, the veterinarian will inject the dog with a sedative to make them sleepy, calm, and comfortable.

Second, the veterinarian will inject a special drug that will peacefully stop their heart.

These drugs work in such a way that the dog will not experience any awareness whatsoever that their life is ending. What they will experience is very similar to falling asleep, or what we humans experience when going under anesthesia during a surgical procedure.

Once the second stage drug has been injected, the entire process takes about 10 to 20 seconds, at which time the veterinarian will then check to make certain that the dog's heart has stopped.

There is no suffering with this process, which is a very gentle and humane way to end a dog's suffering and allows them to peacefully pass on.

We humans are often tempted to delay the inevitable moment of euthanasia, because we love our dogs so much and cannot bear the thought of the intense grief we know will overwhelm us when we must say our final goodbyes to our beloved companion.

Unfortunately, we may regret that we allowed our dog to suffer too long, and find ourselves wishing that we humans had the option to peacefully let go when we reach such a stage in our own lives.

Grieving a Lost Pet

Some humans have difficulty fully recognizing the terrible grief involved in losing a beloved canine friend.

There will be many who do not understand the close bond we humans can have with our dogs, which is often unlike any we have with our human counterparts.

Your friends may give you pitying looks and try to cheer you up, but if they have never experienced the loss of such a special connection themselves, they may also secretly think you are making too much fuss over "just a dog."

For some of us humans, the loss of a beloved dog is so painful that we decide never to share our lives with another, because the thought of going through the pain of such a loss is unbearable.

Expect to feel terribly sad, tearful, and yes, depressed, because those who are close to their canine companions will feel their loss no less acutely than the loss of a human friend or life partner.

The grieving process can take some time to recover from, and some of us never totally recover.

After the loss of a family dog, first you need to take care of yourself by making certain that you remember to eat regular meals and get enough sleep, even though you will feel an almost eerie sense of loneliness.

Losing a beloved dog is a shock to the system that can also affect your concentration and your ability to find joy, or be interested in participating in other activities that are a normal part of your daily life.

Other dogs, cats, and pets in the home will also be grieving the loss of a companion, and may display this by acting depressed, being off their food or showing little interest in play or games.

Therefore, you need to help guide your other pets through this grieving process by keeping them busy and interested, taking them for extra walks and finding ways to spend more time with them.

Wait Long Enough

Many people do not wait long enough before attempting to replace a lost pet and will immediately go to the local shelter and rescue a deserving dog. While this may help to distract you from your grieving process, this is not really fair to the new fur member of your family.

Bringing a new pet into a home that is depressed and grieving the loss of a long-time canine member may create behavioral problems for the new dog that will be faced with learning all about their new home, while also dealing with the unstable energy of the grieving family.

A better scenario would be to allow yourself the time to properly grieve by waiting a minimum of one month to allow yourself and your family to feel happier and more stable before deciding upon sharing your home with another dog.

Managing Health Care Costs

The estimated annual cost for keeping a medium-sized dog, including required health care, is around $650 / £387.

There is, of course, no possible way to estimate the cost of emergency care, advanced procedures, or consultations with specialists.

For this reason, there is a growing interest in pet insurance to help defray the costs of veterinary care. Treatments for our pets are growing in both sophistication and rate of success, but, as is the case with human medical care, the costs can be high.

It may be possible to obtain comprehensive pet insurance including coverage for accidents, illness, and even some hereditary and chronic conditions for as little as $25 / £16.25 per month. Benefit caps and deductibles vary by company.

Afterword

Now that you've spent some time reading about French Bulldogs and learning the basics of their husbandry, I hope you have enough information to decide if this is the breed for you.

Of course, I'll give you my standard advice on any breed — go to a dog show and see some Frenchies for yourself, but be warned, all it takes is one meeting with a round-bellied, baby French Bulldog and you'll probably be hooked for life.

Photo Credit: Kathi Liebe of Starcreek Frenchies

No matter how cute, however, no breed should be adopted based on appearance alone. French Bulldogs have very specific needs in terms of their environment, the level of exercise they can tolerate, and the range of physical ailments to which they are prone.

They are wonderful, loyal, social companionable dogs on the one hand and snorting, farting, stubborn little tyrants on the other. It's hard to explain until you've lived with one that, somewhere in the middle of all of that, may well be the best dog you've ever known — but it's true.

Frenchies are an excellent size to live in an urban environment where even their low exercise needs match the limitations of apartment dwelling. They aren't bad to bark, but they do suffer from all kinds of separation anxiety.

I live successfully with a French Bulldog because I work from home, but if I didn't have a friend to come in and stay with my little guy when I'm away on business, we'd have a serious problem.

You can certainly appreciate and love a breed and still walk away from a potential adoption and say, "That just won't work." Unless you can give a French Bulldog the highest standard of care, including your time and attention, that's exactly what you need to do.

Just as kennel owners should only raise dogs for the love of the breed and with an intention to improve the line, a prospective dog owner should only consider the adoption from the vantage point of the dog's welfare. I always say that if you do right by a Frenchie, he will do right by you. But please, don't do these little guys wrong because they will suffer far more than you will.

Bonus Chapter 1 - Interview with a Champion Breeder

I hope you have enjoyed reading this guide on French Bulldogs and we are not quite finished yet. This extra section is an interview which I did with expert breeder Stephen Miller of Péché Mignon French Bulldogs.

You've come a long way, but just how did your interest in French Bulldogs start?

My interest in Frenchies started when I happened to be driving by the local animal shelter and outside there was a woman holding the most unusual looking dog. I stopped the car and asked her what breed it was. It was, of course, a French Bulldog.

It turns out it was her dog and she worked at the shelter. I went straight home and started doing research on the breed. My first actual Frenchie was a rescue. Chloe is now 8 years old and still doing well.

Most owners will be just that — how did you progress from owner to becoming a top breeder?

After having a French bulldog for a while most owners start to wonder if they are really the owner or the other way around. Frenchies have a way of wrapping you around their front paw and stealing your heart.

Going from having one rescue Frenchie to a top breeder has been a long but rewarding road. Like anything worth doing or having there is a great deal of effort involved. I began by attending dog shows to see "show" examples of the breed and to get to know some of the breeders.

I got my first show dog "Huxley" about two years after getting my first rescue Frenchie Chloe. After finishing him as a champion, things sort of snow-balled. As show folks started to see me on a regular basis more doors began to open up. This allowed me to get Nana, the girl who is my foundation bitch. By studying pedigrees and planning careful breedings, I had some very successful litters with Nana. I am now working with her grandchildren in my breeding program.

Some words of advicè to those thinking about getting in to breeding: If you do it right, don't expect to make money. I am happy if I break even at the end of any given year. Start with the best dogs you can find because, if you don't, you will always be playing catch up with your breeding program.

Find a reliable mentor and work closely with them. Health test your dogs to make sure you are raising dogs that conform to the standard but are also healthy. There are too many Frenchies with health problems as it is.

And now you also show your dogs, how did it start for you and when?

Showing dogs was just a logical byproduct of breeding. I started going to shows to see quality examples of the breed. I started to show my dogs to prove the quality of the dogs I bred.

Can you offer any advice to others who may be wondering if they can also start showing?

My advice to folks who are interested in starting to show: Go to several shows and watch the dogs in the ring. Talk to the folks at the sidelines, most are very happy to talk dogs with you. Find a successful show person to evaluate the dog you plan to start showing.

Don't be disappointed if you don't win. Don't be mad at the winners or let losing spoil your day ... after all it is just a dog show. Find a class on how to show your dog and attend it regularly. Most local Kennel Clubs offer these classes at very reasonable rates.

In terms of your experience in breeding Frenchies, I see there are a lot of breeders selling colors that are not officially recognized by the American Kennel Club, what is your opinion on these Frenchies?

 My issues with non-recognized colors are as follows: Many of these colors can carry health issues related to the color, example ... many all-white Frenchies can be born deaf. To get some of these odd colors other breeds may have been crossed in to the Frenchies to pick up the color gene.

Folks raising dogs in these "fad" colors do so exclusively to make money, plain and simple. They charge ridiculously high prices for their puppies and these puppies are inherently unhealthy.

The colors in the standard are there for a reason, a committee of knowledgeable folks came up with the standard. I think it should be followed for the good of the breed.

Can you offer advice to people looking to buy a Frenchie?

Buying a Frenchie puppy is like playing in a mine field. Don't walk in to the field unless you know EXACTLY where those mines are.

NEVER, repeat, NEVER buy a puppy from a newspaper advertisement or pet store. The price of the puppy may be lower than from a reputable breeder but you will most likely spend many-fold the money you saved there at the veterinarian's office.

Speak with several breeders and find one that you feel comfortable with. You could very well have a ten-year plus relationship with the breeder. Don't get a puppy just because it is close to you. Expect to drive several hours to get your puppy if that breeder seems to be the right one for you.

Always go to the breeder's home and see the conditions your puppy was raised in. Ask to see the parents — at least the mother should be at their home. A red flag should pop up when you see breeders who are willing to ship a puppy and those that take credit cards or PayPal. Breeders who will not let you come to their home should be avoided at all costs. If the breeder does not health test their breeding dogs, RUN THE OTHER WAY.

Answers such as "I know they are healthy" or "they have not had any health issues" are not a substitute for health testing. The parent's health test results should be posted on the various health testing organizations' websites.

At minimum, health testing of the parents should consist of hips, patellas, cardiac, and juvenile cataracts. Bonus testing would be the addition of thyroid, elbows, trachea, and spine. Go to the AKC or your national Kennel Club website and search their list of breeders. Often times these breeders will be reputable. BE PREPARED TO WAIT FOR THE RIGHT PUPPY. Don't feel pressured to buy the first or even the tenth puppy you see.

Are there things that you see owners doing that frustrate you?

The most frustrating thing to me about owners are those who will not educate themselves about the breed and the requirements this breed absolutely must have.

Frenchies thrive on human interaction. Don't get a Frenchie unless you have the time to spend with it. Know the health concerns and be prepared to make informed choices on keeping your dog healthy. Heat is deadly to them ... do not leave them out in warm weather. Any day over 75 degrees could potentially prove fatal to a Frenchie left out or allowed to exert itself too much. Don't leave your Frenchie unattended, even in a fenced yard. These dogs are stolen all of the time.

How should new owners approach bringing a new puppy home? For example, where should the puppy sleep and do you recommend using a crate? Any other advice and tips you can give?

A new puppy is a joy but it is a joy that comes with work and responsibility. Frenchies are difficult to housebreak. Positive reinforcement plus a strictly adhered to schedule is the key to house breaking a Frenchie. Puppies need to be put out to use the bathroom after they eat, after every nap, and at least once an hour when they are awake.

Limit their area of play initially to a room with easy to clean flooring. I really recommend crate training your Frenchie. I do not recommend leaving them in crates for extended periods of time. Crates are not a substitute for interaction and attention.

Don't expect any house breaking miracles until your puppy is about 5 to 6 months old. I like to have the puppy's crate in your bedroom so you can hear if your puppy is having issues during the night.

NEVER feed your puppy and walk away. Sit with them until they are done. Many Frenchies have choked to death while owners were in the other room while their dog ate. Do not leave food with them in their crates, or toys that they can easily tear apart and ingest.

Never give soft things such as rawhide, "Greenies" etc. to your Frenchie. They are a huge choke hazard. Always think "hard and or crunchy" when it comes to toys and treats.

Deer antlers are wonderful toys for Frenchies. They last a long time and do not splinter. Always introduce a new puppy slowly to adult dogs in your home. Feed the puppy separately from any adult dogs.

What feeding routines and types of food/supplements do you recommend?

For puppies under 6 months of age I recommend free feeding. Basically let them eat as much as they want. When they hit 6 months, start to feed them twice per day, somewhere between 3/4 to 1 cup at each feeding. If your puppy looks thin, feed more than this. Always feed a high quality grain-free food. Some folks feed a raw diet and, from what I have seen, the raw diets work well. A puppy vitamin once a day is fine as a supplement.

Are French Bulldogs hard or easy to train?

Yes, Frenchies are hard to train. I tell folks that if you want a dog that listens to you, get a Golden Retriever. Frenchies are stubborn, without a doubt. Accept this and you and your Frenchie will have a wonderful relationship.

To me, getting a Frenchie and expecting them to do everything you ask them to, the minute you ask them to, is like buying rabbit and expecting it to fly. You will only be disappointed. If you can deal with a dog that thinks they are on the same social level as you, get a Frenchie. If you can deal with a dog that wants to be with you most all of the time, get a Frenchie.

Thanks so much Stephen for sharing your expertise and just for sharing your unique story with everyone.

Stephen Miller of Péché Mignon French Bulldogs
http://www.pechemignonfrenchbulldogs.com

Bonus Chapter 2 - Interview with an Expert Show Dog Owner

Our second guest chapter is a special interview I did with Karen Fore-Monroe, who is a contributor to this book.

Karen, thanks for doing this interview, can you tell us who you are and where you are based?

I am Karen Fore of Tecumseh, Oklahoma, USA, and breeder of Fancibul French Bulldogs since my first acquaintance with a French bulldog in 1992.

My deceased husband (Bob Fore) and I have owner-handled many dogs to attain AKC titles until his last few years when his health was declining. We then used professional handler services for a few years.

Recently, I remarried and have moved to a new location on the outskirts of metropolitan Oklahoma City, Oklahoma, where I was born.

My current husband has had a beautiful kennel facility built right outside our kitchen door. There are two large fenced play yards and a smaller one for puppies, large indoor-outdoor runs, and a beautiful view of the city.

I wanted to interview you because it seems to me you have an interesting personal story to tell given your success showing your French Bulldogs.

Perhaps we could start by you telling us what achievements you have just accomplished?

I am excited to again owner handle two young bitches and a puppydog, because I've been "out of the ring" for most of 2013-2014, although we did acquire a title on one bitch in 2014. In my comeback to the show ring, I was awarded Winner's Bitch, Best of Winner, Best Opposite Sex, and Best of Breed Owner-Handled.

Bob and I bred 67 puppies that achieved championships in America and other countries, primarily in AKC conformation competitions, although some have obedience and rally titles.

Some have dual championships in AKC and other countries, such as Russia, Taiwan, Thailand, Argentina, Brazil, and Canada.

Bootsie (in my second show ring experience) achieved a Canadian and AKC title as Can. Am Ch Fancibuls Boots Scooter. He left us to live his life in Argentina where he received a L. Am Intl title and became an important foundation for many pedigrees of show breeders in South American countries.

I'm sure a lot of readers think there's lots of mystery behind these dog shows, but how did it start for you and when?

When I made my declaration to "get one, learn to show it, and breed it so others can know how wonderful they are," it was a heartfelt commitment.

There were few French bulldogs and few breeders in 1992. It was an expensive and persistent search before I found my first French bulldog with a notable pedigree from an ethical show breeder.

Alas, this one had a beautiful pedigree of five generations of AKC champions, but was shy and somewhat "fear aggressive." It took me 8 months to get her to move on a lead. I had "leadbroken" dogs a few times but never ran into such resistance.

I WAS EVEN LESS THAN NOVICE but did show this bitch 3 times at a few small shows and acquired a few points. After a few years of struggling with her, I gave up on her ever accepting dog showing, although I have yet to have many dogs over these years as intelligent as this female.

My next two bitches lacked in temperament, although one became a champion. Such struggle led to my determination to focus on temperament in my breeding program. If the dog is not adaptable and does not meet the standard for breed temperament, it is difficult to successfully show-off, and it is not the best for daily family lifestyle either.

From my first litter in 1994, I kept a male. When he was 6 months, I took him into the showring. With all the hands-on attention this puppy had received, he had become quite the little precocious clown, rather boisterous at times, never shy and often "out of control" on his lead. The judge abruptly took the lead from my hand and remarked, "here is how you hold the lead so you can control your dog."

As the class judging moved along, we improved, and he won Winners Dog. There were several titled dogs in the competition, but the judge gave my cobby puppy "Best of Breed" which was a whopping 5 point major win, the ultimate number of points in the AKC conformation competitions.

Leaving the ring, I learned there was another event called "Variety Group Judging." I had never seen a variety group. A lady at ringside stepped up and remarked, "this is the best French bulldog I've seen in years, would you let me take him into the groups for you?" I did.

She is still a close girlfriend and was a matron of honor for my recent wedding. With her advice, watching other handlers show dogs, attending real handling/training classes, and acquiring more experience, I became accomplished at training and handling. My husband also began handling our dogs at times, and Bob finished many for us and other breeder-friends.

I know a lot of readers of this book are just interested in owning a French Bulldog and may not necessarily want to show their dogs, but to anybody who is interested, is it an impossible dream or can anybody start to show?

Nobody could start out with less knowledge of dogs, dog training, and dog show events than I did. I've made many blunders as I learned, but I've also heard others share their embarrassing moments and blunders. Even trained professional handlers admit they have had their embarrassing moments in the showring.

Therefore, I wholeheartedly encourage others to participate in the Sport of Dogs. I truly believe if someone with my lack of knowledge and skill could accomplish what has been accomplished in the past 20 years, anybody can.

In the mid-90's, my husband and I lived in a rural area without information highway nor any mentors. Times have changed. Breeders are encouraged to mentor those that are interested in the Sport of Dogs. Kennel clubs have dog training conformation and obedience classes in many areas. Information is readily available through local and national kennel clubs, The American Kennel Club registry, and the Internet.

The American Kennel Club has in recent years created an "Amateur Owner Handler" class in which newbies can exhibit, and even a variety group judging event just for owner handlers.

I certainly encourage every new owner to give the Sport of Dogs a try. I am always available to encourage and advise, help novices strategize, and at times say, "hang in there" because there are "highs and lows"; but, BEWARE, this sport is addictive to some!

Thanks Karen for sharing your expertise and for sharing your unique story with everyone.

Karen Fore-Monroe of Fancibul French Bulldogs
http://www.fancibul.com

Bonus Chapter 3 - Owners of Sir Charles Barkley

This extra section is an interview which I did with Paul and Melissa, owners of one of the most famous French Bulldogs in the world, Sir Charles Barkley.

Thanks for doing this interview, can you tell us who you are and where you live?

We're Paul and Melissa and we own Sir Charles Barkley (@barkleysircharles on Instagram) the French Bulldog. We live in Seattle, Washington.

How long have you owned Barkley?

We've owned Barkley since he was over 10 weeks old, so over 2 years now.

Where did you buy him/her from?

We researched local breeders because we wanted to know where he came from. We were able to visit him every two weeks at the breeders until the day we brought him home. We also met his mom and dad and all his siblings.

How on earth has Barkley become such a well-known French Bulldog, I believe he now has over 200,000 followers on Instagram?

Sometimes we're not even sure! We started his account just for fun and all of a sudden his numbers started jumping and he was being featured on websites.

We think he has a distinct look. He's small, but chunky, with a big head and big eyes. And somehow that all fits well with his goofy personality.

We know celebrities have many issues with fame, how is Barkley handling the attention!?

We think Barkley thought he was a celebrity as soon as he was born! He absolutely loves attention. He sees people, runs up to them, and squats down already expecting a back rub.

Why do you think people should choose the French Bulldog over another breed of dog?

Not sure about other people but it's all about preference. We chose a French Bulldog because, at the time, we were living in a smaller home without much of a yard so we knew we couldn't get a big dog that needs tons of exercise.

We were actually deciding between Frenchies and Corgi's but when we called Barkley's breeder and said they had a litter born that day, we knew that was it!

There seems to be some debate over nutrition and feeding, what are your routines, such as how often and what types of food do you feed Barkley?

We know a lot of Frenchies who have food allergies. In time, you'll just have to eliminate items that cause your Frenchie problems and ask your vet too.

Barkley is on a vet-prescribed diet and we believe he's done so much better on it. His coat is better, goes "potty" regularly, and less gassy!

Obviously grooming is another major aspect of owning a French Bulldog, can you offer any tips, advice and perhaps some accessories, that you wouldn't be without?

We do lots to keep Barkley looking groomed. We give him a bath every other week, or depending on how much he's played outside. We make sure his face folds are dry and clean every day or else tear stains will develop. We just use unscented baby wipes and go through them like he's a newborn baby.

We wipe his paws, private areas after he's done his business, and clean his face. We try to brush him weekly since he definitely sheds a lot.

Follow Sir Charles Barkley:
instagram.com/barkleysircharles
https://www.facebook.com/BarkleySC

Bonus Chapter 4 - Westminster Dog Show Winner Interview

While this book is aimed at pet owners, many people go on to develop such a love of the Frenchie that they want to show their dog off. We are privileged to interview Necia Metzger of Metzger's Bulldogs who won Best of Breed at the famous Westminster Dog Show.

Necia, most owners would dream of taking part in the Westminster Dog Show, but to win such a prestigious award, how does that feel?

It was the most exciting event of my life as a breeder and exhibitor, and the highlight of 43 years in the show ring. I was on cloud nine!

When you went to the show did you have the hope or aim of winning?

I had never entered a dog at Westminster before and I was hoping for an Award of Merit. To attain that alone would have put me over the moon.

What is it like to take part? Perhaps you could give us an insider's view behind the scenes?

I used a handler, Esteban Farias, but I was at ringside, enjoying every moment, with my fingers crossed for an award.

To take Breed was a shock! I knew Jagger was that good, but would the judge, Dr. Reppond, see it?

After Jagger's win, I cried tears of joy for two solid hours because it meant so much to me.

How does an owner get to take part in the Westminster Dog Show — where do they start out?

You should start your journey to a win like this by finding a great mentor in your breed. Mine was, and still is, Jan Galiszewski at Joy French Bulldogs.

After that you begin to study, study, study the breed standard as set down by the parent club. Also, familiarize yourself with the pedigrees of the top winning and producing kennels in the country.

Finally, begin your breeding program with healthy, good tempered stock that fits that standard as closely as possible.

As an expert, what advice would you give to people who are looking to buy a French Bulldog?

As harsh as it may sound, any seller's word is only as good as the written contract and its conditions and promises. We all fall in "puppy love," but we need to lead with our brain and common sense and not just with our heart.

What don't you like to see French Bulldogs owners doing?

Sometimes owners, particularly pet owners, forget that dogs are just like children. They need strict guidelines and structure with equal heaps of love and gentle discipline.

What advice concerning types of food would you give owners?

Use whatever food works for your dog! A dog's digestive system, skin, and physical make-up are as varied as ours is from person to person. We don't all eat the same with the same results, so why should the dogs'?

Don't be fooled by fancy ads, inflated prices, and scare tactics. Remember, all commercial foods for dogs have USFDA approval.

Are there any special tips and items that you can share or recommend?

Do preventative maintenance on your dog's eyes, ears, skin, and coat regularly. It will save you and your dog from many problems. Be pro-active with the dog's health.

Are there any final thoughts that you feel the readers of this book would benefit from?

The French Bulldog is a wonderful breed. Having said that, each prospective buyer should carefully study the breed to determine if this breed truly fits their lifestyle and needs.

It is a huge commitment to bring these dogs into your home and should be done soberly and thoughtfully.

Thank you Necia for answering our questions on behalf of our readers.

Necia Metzger of Metzger's Bulldogs
http://metzgersfrenchbulldogs.com/

Appendix - Breed Standard – United Kingdom

General Appearance - Sturdy, compact solid, small dog with good bone, short, smooth coat. No point exaggerated, balance essential. Dogs showing respiratory distress highly undesirable.

Characteristics - Full of courage, yet with clown-like qualities. Bat ears and short tail characteristic features of the breed.

Temperament - Vivacious, deeply affectionate, intelligent.

Head and Skull - Head square in appearance and in proportion to dog's size. Skull nearly flat between ears, domed forehead. The skin covering the skull and forehead should be supple enough to allow fine wrinkling when the dog is alert.

Well defined muzzle, broad, deep and set back, muscles of cheeks well developed. Stop well defined. Lower jaw deep, square, broad, slightly undershot and turned up. Nose black and wide, relatively short, with open nostrils and line between well defined.

Lips black, thick, meeting each other in centre, completely hiding teeth. Upper lip covers lower on each side with plenty of cushion, never so exaggerated as to hang too much below level of lower jaw.

Eyes - Preferably dark and matching. Moderate size, round, neither sunken nor prominent, showing no white when looking straight forward; set relatively wide apart and on same level as the stop.

Ears - 'Bat ears', of medium size, wide at base, rounded at top; set high, carried upright and parallel, a sufficient width of skull preventing them being too close together; skin soft and fine, orifice as seen from the front, showing entirely. The opening to the ear canal should be wide and open.

Mouth - Slightly undershot. Teeth sound and regular, but not visible when the mouth is closed. Tongue must not protrude.

Neck - Powerful, well arched and thick, of moderate length. Forequarters Legs set wide apart, straight boned, strong, muscular and short.

Body - Cobby, muscular and well-rounded with deep wide brisket and ribs well sprung. Strong, gently roached back. Good 'cut up'. The body while broader at the shoulders should narrow slightly beyond the ribs to give definition to the relatively short, thick, strong, muscular loin.

Hindquarters - Legs strong, muscular and relatively longer than forelegs with moderate angulation. Absolute soundness essential. Hocks well let down.

Feet - Small, compact and placed in continuation of line of leg, with absolutely sound pasterns. Hind feet rather longer than the fore-feet. Toes compact; well knuckled; nails short, thick and preferably black.

Tail - Undocked, short, set low, thick at root, tapering quickly towards tip, preferably straight and long enough to cover anus, never curling over back nor carried gaily.

Gait/Movement - Free and flowing. Soundness of movement of the utmost importance.

Colour - Brindle, pied or fawn. Tan, mouse and grey/blue highly undesirable. Brindle: a mixture of black and coloured hairs. May contain white provided brindle predominates.

Pied: white predominates over brindle. Whites are classified with pieds for show purposes; but their eyelashes and eye rims should be black. In pieds the white should be clear with definite brindle patches and no ticking or black spots. Fawn: may contain brindle hairs but must have black eye lashes and eye rims.

Coat - Texture fine, smooth, lustrous, short and close.

Size - Ideal weight: dogs: 12.5 kgs (28 lbs); bitches: 11 kgs (24 lbs). Soundness not to be sacrificed to smallness.

Faults - Any departure from the foregoing points should be considered a fault and the seriousness with which the fault should be regarded should be in exact proportion to its degree and its effect upon the health and welfare of the dog.

Photo Credit: Mary Schroeder of FleetFire French Bulldogs

Glossary

Abdomen – The surface area of a dog's body lying between the chest and the hindquarters, also referred to as the belly.

Allergy – An abnormally sensitive reaction to substances including pollens, foods, or microorganisms. May be present in humans or animals with similar symptoms including, but not limited to, sneezing, itching, and skin rashes.

Anal glands – Glands located on either side of a dog's anus used to mark territory. May become blocked and require treatment by a veterinarian.

Arm – On a dog, the region between the shoulder and the elbow is referred to as the arm or the upper arm.

Artificial Insemination – The process by which semen is artificially introduced into the reproductive tract of a female dog for the purposes of a planned pregnancy.

Back – That portion of a dog's body that extends from the withers (or shoulder) to the croup (approximately the area where the back flows into the tail).

Backyard Breeder – Any person engaged in the casual breeding of purebred dogs with no regard to genetic quality or consideration of the breed standard is referred to as a backyard breeder.

Bat Ear – A dog's ear that stands upright from a broad base with a rounded top and a forward-facing opening.

Bitch – The appropriate term for a female dog.

Blooded – An accepted reference to a pedigreed dog.

Breed – A line or race of dogs selected and cultivated by man from a common gene pool to achieve and maintain a characteristic appearance and function.

Breed Standard – A written "picture" of a perfect specimen of a given breed in terms of appearance, movement, and behavior as formulated by a parent organization, for example, the American Kennel Club or in Great Britain, The Kennel Club.

Brindle - A marking pattern typically described in conjunction with another color to achieve a layering of black hairs with a lighter color (fawn, brown, or gray) to produce a tiger-striped pattern.

Brows – The contours of the frontal bone that form ridges above a dog's eyes.

Buttocks – The hips or rump of a dog.

Castrate – The process of removing a male dog's testicles.

Chest – That portion of a dog's trunk or body encased by the ribs.

Coat – The hair covering a dog. Most breeds have both an outer coat and an undercoat.

Come into Season – The point at which a female dog becomes fertile for purposes of mating.

Congenital – Any quality, particularly an abnormality, present at birth.

Crate – Any portable container used to house a dog for transport or provided to a dog in the home as a "den."

Crossbred – Dogs are said to be crossbred when each of their parents is of a different breed.

Dam – A term for the female parent.

Dew Claw – The dew claw is an extra claw on the inside of the leg. It is a rudimentary fifth toe.

Euthanize – The act of relieving the suffering of a terminally ill animal by inducing a humane death, typically with an overdose of anesthesia.

Fancier – Any person with an exceptional interest in purebred dogs and the shows where they are exhibited.

Free Feeding – The practice of making a constant supply of food available for a dog's consumption. Not recommended with French Bulldogs.

Groom – To make a dog's coat neat by brushing, combing, or trimming.

Harness - A cloth or leather strap shaped to fit the shoulders and chest of a dog with a ring at the top for attaching a lead. An alternative to using a collar.

Haunch Bones – Terminology for the hip bones of a dog.

Haw – The membrane inside the corner of a dog's eye known as the third eyelid.

Head - The cranium and muzzle of a dog.

Hip Dysplasia – A condition in dogs due to a malformation of the hip resulting in painful and limited movement degrees.

Hindquarters – The back portion of a dog's body including the pelvis, thighs, hocks, and paws.

Hock – Bones on the hind leg of a dog that form the joint between the second thigh and the metatarsus. Known as the dog's true heel.

Inbreeding – When two dogs of the same breed, that are closely related, mate.

Kennel – A facility where dogs are housed for breeding or an enclosure where dogs are kept.

Lead – Any strap, cord, or chain used to restrain or lead a dog. Typically attached to a collar or harness. Also called a leash.

Litter – The puppy or puppies from a single birth or "whelping."

Muzzle – That portion of a dog's head lying in front of the eyes and consisting of the nasal bone, nostrils, and jaws.

Neuter - To castrate or spay a dog thus rendering them incapable of reproducing.

Pedigree - The written record of a pedigreed dog's genealogy. Should extend to three or more generations.

Puppy – Any dog of less than 12 months of age.

Puppy Mill – An establishment that exists for the purpose of breeding as many puppies for sale as possible with no consideration of potential genetic defects.

Rose Ear – Small ears that fold over and back revealing the burr.

Separation Anxiety – The anxiety and stress suffered by a dog left alone for any period of time.

Sire – The accepted term for the male parent.

Spay – The surgery to remove a female dog's ovaries to prevent conception.

Whelping – Term for the act of giving birth to puppies.

Withers – The highest point of a dog's shoulders.

Wrinkle – Any folding and loose skin on the forehead and foreface of a dog.

Photo Credit: Susan L. Neidlinger of Crusader French Bulldogs

Index